THE LOTUS AND THE STARS

The Way of Astro-Yoga

ROB AND TRISH MACGREGOR

Contemporary Books
Chicago New York San Francisco Lisbon London Madrid Mexico City
Milan New Delhi San Juan Seoul Singapore Sydney Toronto

Library of Congress Cataloging-in-Publication Data

MacGregor, Rob.
The lotus and the stars : the way of astro-yoga / Rob and Trish MacGregor.
p. cm.
Includes index.
ISBN 0-8092-9895-3
1. Astrology. 2. Yoga—Miscellanea. I. MacGregor, T. J. II. Title.

BF1729.Y64 M23 2001
133.5—dc21 00-48393

Contemporary Books

A Division of The ***McGraw-Hill*** *Companies*

1 2 3 4 5 6 7 8 9 0 VL/VL 0 9 8 7 6 5 4 3 2 1

ISBN 0-8092-9895-3

This book was set in ACaslon Regular by Hespenheide Design
Printed and bound by Vicks Lithograph

Cover design by Monica Baziuk
Cover Illustrations: *Front, clockwise from top* © Dover, © Mia Klein/Photonica, © Dover, © Dover, © Bettmann/Corbis. *Back, right* © Bettmann/Corbis, *all others* © Dover
Interior design by Hespenheide Design

The authors would like to extend many thanks to yoga teachers Anne Laure Michelis and Cherie Carson for their generous time spent posing for the photographs in this book.

This book is printed on acid-free paper.

For Megan with love

Contents

I

Introducing Astro~Yoga

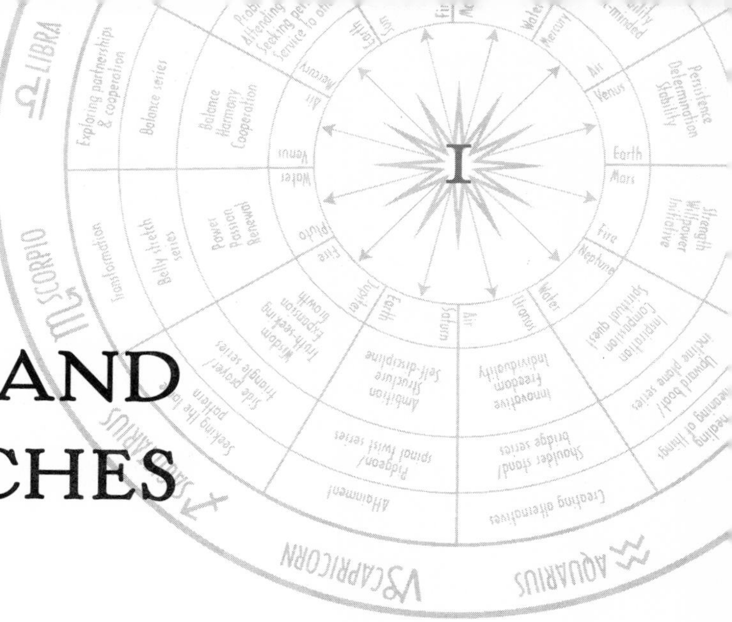

I

Stars and Stretches

You've had a bad day, a Murphy's Law sort of day, where everything that could possibly go wrong did go wrong. You're in desperate need of energy, ambition, and a spiritual boost. So you shut the door to your office, kick off your shoes, change into comfortable clothes, and proceed through a series of yoga postures designed to give you the energy of Aries, the ambition of Capricorn, and the spiritual insight of Pisces.

Welcome to the world of Astro-Yoga, where the energies of the sun signs and the planets are drawn into your body through specific yoga postures, so that your body ultimately becomes a vehicle for transforming your life. Sound improbable? Then let's get specific.

Suppose that on this Murphy's Law sort of day you're going to give a presentation to a new client, and what you will need most is magnetism. The sign of Leo is all about magnetism, and since it's ruled by the sun, the sun salutation will help you shine. Leo also rules the heart—the fourth energy center—so you should particularly emphasize the back-bending portion of the sequence. This movement will allow you to give your presentation "from the heart."

Or perhaps you're in a situation where you need to forge ahead, doing what you think is right even if everyone around you says you're wrong. In this case, it would be helpful to draw in some of the fearlessness of Aries, the sign that lives life like the "Star Trek" motto, boldly going where no one has gone before. Since Aries is ruled by Mars, the god of war, the warrior posture would be helpful in bringing in the energy you need.

Every sun sign is an archetype, a blueprint for particular characteristics that distinguish it from other signs. Geminis are known for their mental agility, Aries for their energy. Scorpios are intense and sexual, Sagittarians are truth seekers. Virgos are detail-oriented, Leos shine on center stage. Every sign manifests a particular *archetypal energy* based, in part, on the planet that rules that sign. These are the energies that Astro-Yoga postures tap.

Form and Intent

Perhaps you already practice yoga and have done the sun salutation thousands of times, but have never associated it with personal magnetism. Part of the reason may be that you have never practiced Astro-Yoga, which involves *intent* as well as form. Form involves working on the physical challenge of a posture, while intent attracts the energy associated with the posture and its related astrological sign.

Yoga is a Sanskrit term which means yoke—union of the body, mind, and soul. By combining yoga with astrological energies, you become more aware of the intimate connections between your physical self and your emotions, mind, and spirit. This awareness, in turn, empowers you. And once you're empowered, you're better able to sculpt and mold your life to fit what you want and need.

Benefits and Advantages of Astro-Yoga

While astrology provides a blueprint for your life, Astro-Yoga illustrates how to apply the lessons and provides an active vehicle for making changes in your life. Most traditional yoga practices serve as an excellent means of letting go of the outside world for a period of time. Astro-Yoga, however, differs in that it integrates the "outside" and the "inside." It allows you not only to recharge but also to prepare for your daily life by giving you an opportunity to remake your life as you want to live it.

In Astro-Yoga, it is *not* necessary to have your astrological chart available to fully benefit from the practice. As long as you know your own sun sign, you're able to personalize your workout. The workouts vary in length according to your needs. If you're short on time and want to focus on one particular area, an Astro-Yoga workout can be squeezed into fifteen or twenty minutes.

For decades, yoga carried a stigma of being too Eastern, too weird, linked to the world of gurus and devoted followers. In Astro-Yoga, you become your own guru. Once you learn the system, you can create your own workout and alter it as your needs change. It can be practiced alone or in a group. It also serves as a great personal addendum to yoga classes that you might take at a yoga studio or fitness center. While you may be only able to get to a yoga class once or twice a week, you can practice Astro-Yoga at home on a daily basis.

The Birth of Astro-Yoga

Astro-Yoga is a unique type of yoga that was born during a full moon in the mid-1990s. For years, we joked that our separate interests in astrology and yoga fit our particular sun signs, Gemini and Taurus. Gemini, an air sign, tends to be attracted to mental pursuits; Taurus, an earth sign, is definitely more physical. Then, on a night of the full moon, Rob was talking about plans to lead a class in the moon salutation and added that he would start out with the more well-known sun salutation. Something clicked.

The mention of the moon and the sun suddenly linked yoga and astrology, and it set off a series of conversations about how the planets and astrological signs were associated with certain body parts, as well as emotional, physical, and mental patterns. We realized that specific yoga postures, related to the signs and planets, could address the needs, conflicts, and challenges that people encounter in their daily lives.

This launched our research and exploration into the areas where yoga and astrology merge. We discovered that, although some yoga teachers refer to planetary influences, no practice existed that combined the two. So we proceeded to adapt many of the traditional postures in various yoga disciplines to the gamut of sun signs. Through trial and error, Astro-Yoga—a merger of the lotus and the stars—was born.

At the time, Trish had been a practicing astrologer for a number of years and had written several books on the subject. Rob, who is also an award-winning writer, had been teaching yoga for several years and had practiced the discipline in various schools of yoga. His own classes were already an amalgam of what he liked best from the different schools, but now he began integrating the principles of Astro-Yoga into them.

Intuitively, we felt that Astro-Yoga had once existed in the distant past. As the saying goes, there's nothing new under the sun; everything that seems new is simply a redefinition of what has already been done. If that's the case, then we are pleased and honored to have had the opportunity to revive, or reinvent, an ancient practice.

In the years since its birth, Astro-Yoga has brought about significant changes in our lives and the lives of the people who are practicing it. As one Aries man says, "It's one thing to do yoga postures for flexibility, strength, and a general sense of well-being, but it's empowering to know that I can use my *intent* to determine the kind of energy I pull in. It has allowed me to live more consciously."

Hatha Yoga

The first part of an Astro-Yoga workout deals with *form*—the postures (or *asanas*) themselves. The second part focuses on *intent*—using the postures to pull in specific types of energy.

In form, the focus remains on the body and posture as well as on how you breathe. The practice of yoga postures, known generically as hatha yoga, increases flexibility and strength. Muscles are toned and lengthened, making them leaner and more supple. Tightness is reduced as connective tissue becomes more pliable and elastic. Yoga can improve your posture, the alignment of the spine, and adjust muscular imbalances. Toxins are removed from the organs, and the entire system is revitalized.

Inverted postures, such as the shoulder stand, headstand, or the standing forward bend, bring more oxygenated blood to the brain cells. This reversal of the flow of blood also strengthens the heart muscle and improves circulation, while other postures improve balance and mental concentration.

The forward bend and the bridge postures, among others, increase the flexibility of the spine. There's a saying, often heard in yoga classes, that you are only as young or as old as your spine is flexible. As your spine, the foundation of your frame, becomes more flexible, so do the connective tissues and muscles attached to it. Your movements become more catlike. Your entire body becomes more flexible and less tense.

Breathing exercises allow the body and mind to relax, make lung tissue more elastic, and massage the internal organs. During relaxation and meditation, blood pressure and stress levels also are lowered.

These benefits can be readily achieved through any yoga practice. With Astro-Yoga, however, the envelope of possibilities is stretched as we move beyond form and into intent, where we draw on energy forces related to the celestial bodies.

Astro-Yoga and the Age of Aquarius

It may seem as if yoga and astrology are two distinct disciplines: one, a study of the patterns of the celestial bodies and how they relate to our lives; the other, a physical discipline that affects the mind and spirit. Even in Eastern cultures, where both disciplines have long been accepted, they have traditionally been approached as two separate practices. Yet, the connections between astrology and yoga are readily apparent. Hatha yoga relates to the ability to act and reflect. *Ha* is symbolized by the sun, a celestial body which is the warm, creative, physical side of our being. *Tha* is symbolized by another celestial body, the moon, which is the cool, receptive, emotional, and intuitive side of our personalities. Practicing yoga harmonizes the two parts and brings the right and left hemispheres of our brains into synch.

More directly, astrology and yoga are linked through *prana*, a Sanskrit word for life force or life current. Prana, drawn in when we inhale, circulates through the body, sustaining and connecting body, mind, and energy. While prana is carried by the breath, it is much more than simply oxygen. It is a vital universal force that supports the mind and body just as it powers the planets and stars. It exists in the air we breathe, the food we eat, and it can be "inhaled" into our beings through our use of *intent*.

Prana moves in the body along *nadis*, or invisible energy channels, which energize the organs and cells. These channels intersect the body at points known as *chakras*, energy centers located at a roughly vertical axis from the tailbone to the crown of the head. In astrology, the chakras are linked to particular planets and sun signs. For instance, the sun and Leo are connected to the fourth chakra, *anahata* in Sanskrit, which is associated with the heart. Venus, which rules Taurus, is connected with the fifth chakra, or *vishuddha*, which is located near the throat.

In traditional yoga, the movement of prana along the chakras is directed in breathing exercises, or *pranayama*, and is sometimes the focus of active meditation. Astro-Yoga adds another level—the use of intent to draw and focus this energy force into our lives.

In astrological terms, the timing is perfect for the emergence of Astro-Yoga. We're at the threshold of the Age of Aquarius, and the archetypal energy of Aquarius—an air sign, a mental sign—is holistic and unifying. It seeks to bring together people of diverse groups and belief systems. The Aquarian energy does this by introducing sudden change and disrupting old thought patterns and paradigms so that new patterns can be born.

Carolyn Myss, author of *Anatomy of the Spirit*, notes that the core perception of the Aquarian Age, the belief that we create our own reality, actually began during the sixties. "This single notion inspired an entirely new view of the potential of human power in every part of human life," she writes. "The corollary of this idea is the belief that we create our own health and can affect our own healing." It is believed that the Aquarian Age, which will last about a thousand years, will usher in a new era of health and wellness. Its energy, Myss writes, "fills us with the sensation that we are exquisitely creative beings with internal resources powerful enough to heal illnesses that have always been considered intractable and to challenge the speed at which we age."

Uranus, ruler of Aquarius, also rules astrology. Uranus, which entered Aquarius in 1996 and will stay there until 2003, ushered us into the new millennium. This astrological influence allows for the expansion of astrology into new realms.

Most astrologers agree that the vibrational rate of the planet and humanity is increasing. Compare the pace of life at the outset of the 21st century with that of the 1950s. Through dramatic advances in communications and technology, we receive vast amounts of information instantly. At the same time, more and more of us are opening up to a greater awareness of who we are, while expanding the limits of our physical and mental capabilities.

Yoga and astrology, both based on ancient traditions, are gaining in popularity and adapting to the new era. Just as astrology changed and adapted with the discovery of Pluto, yoga finds itself in the midst of change under the influences of the Western world and emerging thought patterns. The merger of astrology and yoga in Astro-Yoga signifies another new way of expanding our limits, of finding and following our dreams. Through the practice, we learn from the past, and in doing so we gain access to transformative energy for the future.

2

Getting Aligned

In the moment you drew your first breath, the sun, moon, and other planets stood in a particular spot relative to the earth and the rest of the universe. If you were born on tax day, you're an Aries. A new year's birth would make you a Capricorn. A birth on Halloween would make you a Scorpio.

Sun Signs and Their Characteristics

Astrology teaches that each sun sign possesses specific attributes that characterize it and influence who we are. Aries, ruled by Mars, is aggressive and impatient but also independent and action-oriented. This is hardly a surprise when you look at the role Mars played in classical mythology. He was the god of war, the aggressor, the guy who got things done. This is why when there's work to be done, when there are worlds to discover and pioneer, you want an Aries around.

Sometimes, the planet that rules a particular sign emphasizes an overall theme about the sign rather than the minutiae. Take Pisces, the sign of the dreamer, the mystic, the person who just can't make up her mind. Neptune, the god whose natural element is water, rules Pisces. To live in water is to perceive everything differently, to breathe differently. Where other people walk, Pisces swims. Neptune personifies the Piscean *archetype*, that of a person who *feels* her way through life, relying more heavily on emotions and intuition than intellect. Pisces, like her element, molds herself to the shape of the vessel into which she's poured.

In astrology, one of the ways in which signs are classified is according to the elements—fire, earth, air, and water. Three signs go with each element and, regardless of the often vast differences between signs of the same element, they are bonded by this common element. They're like siblings, united by bloodlines.

The Astro-Yoga postures are linked to these elements—that is, some postures are definitely "fire" postures, others are definitely "water," "earth," or "air." The sun salutation, for example, is linked with Leo, a fire sign, which is ruled by the sun. The warrior posture can be linked only to Aries, which is ruled by the god of war; the moon salutation is clearly linked to Cancer, which is ruled by the moon; and the balance posture series is linked to Libra, which is symbolized by a set of balance scales.

Not every posture is as obvious as these four, but when you look beneath the surface, the connection is there. Take Gemini and the forehead-to-knee series. Gemini is an air sign, a communicator, and is ruled by Mercury. Mercury, the messenger, was constantly on the move, delivering messages from one part of Olympus to the other, or from Olympus to earth. The Gemini series of yoga postures engages the frontal part of the brain, the forehead, with a point of flexibility—the knee. So, in a symbolic and physical sense, the series connects the mind with a flexible attitude—adaptability and versatility, Gemini qualities.

Someone in need of improving communication skills or a more flexible attitude in dealing with others can benefit from the

Gemini postures. Likewise, if you are faced with handling several projects at the same time, you can also benefit from the energy linked to this sign.

In many ways, the postures reflect the basic theme of the particular sun signs. They are the ideal physical expression of the sign's archetype. Even though most people know the sun signs, they are listed here with their appropriate dates. The signs can also be grouped according to elements.

Sun Signs and Dates

Sign	Symbol	Birth Dates
Aries	♈	March 21–April 19
Taurus	♉	April 20–May 20
Gemini	♊	May 21–June 21
Cancer	♋	June 22–July 22
Leo	♌	July 23–August 22
Virgo	♍	August 23–September 22
Libra	♎	September 23–October 22
Scorpio	♏	October 23–November 21
Sagittarius	♐	November 22–December 21
Capricorn	♑	December 22–January 19
Aquarius	♒	January 20–February 18
Pisces	♓	February 19–March 20

Fire Signs (action): Aries, Leo, Sagittarius

Fire signs are characterized by aggression, leadership, and independence. They are spontaneous, blunt, outspoken, and are primarily interested in immediate action. Their enthusiasm is often interpreted as impatience by others, but they are always dynamic, energetic individuals.

Earth Signs (physical): Taurus, Virgo, Capricorn
Pragmatism and efficiency are the hallmarks of earth signs. They excel as organizers and in managing material resources. They are firmly rooted in the here and now and are stable, reliable, dependable, and often security-minded.

Air Signs (mental): Gemini, Libra, Aquarius
Air signs are characterized by their mental and intellectual abilities. They're communicators and have an ease for acquiring and using information. Quite often, they are most concerned with the future rather than the here and now. The world of ideas is their domain.

Water Signs (emotions): Cancer, Scorpio, Pisces
Emotions and intuition are the domain of water signs. They are sensitive, psychic, and receptive. They connect easily to the personal unconscious and have rich inner lives that are usually inscrutable to others.

Modalities and Energy

The next time you're at a party or social gathering, observe the ways in which people interact. In any given group, you're sure to see certain archetypes: the networker, the chameleon, the social butterfly, the prom queen, the jock, the philosopher, the doer, the wallflower, the talker. All of these people are using energy in a specific way.

The networker connects people; the chameleon is so adaptable he or she can fit in virtually anywhere; the philosopher offers a particular set of beliefs. You get the idea. In each instance, these people are expressing certain qualities of their sun signs which, in astrology, are known as modalities. There are three such groupings: cardinal, fixed, and mutable. Four signs fall under each group, and each group holds one sign of each element.

Cardinal signs—Aries, Cancer, Libra, and Capricorn—use energy in a *focused* way. They tend to be outgoing and social and are good at initiating new ideas and projects. They're creators; they plant seeds. Their challenge is to follow things through to completion.

Fixed signs—Taurus, Leo, Scorpio, and Aquarius—use energy in a *resolute* way. They stabilize, sustain, persevere. They seek stability through what the cardinal signs have initiated and tend to be resistant to change. They have fixed opinions and excellent memories. Their challenge is to become more flexible.

Mutable signs—Gemini, Virgo, Sagittarius, and Pisces—use energy by being *adaptable*. They adapt and transform what the fixed signs seek to stabilize. Their focus is knowledge, information, and communication. They are often so changeable, however, that their energy may get scattered in the wind.

In Astro-Yoga, the way we use energy is as vital as the qualities we're seeking to "pull in" through various postures. If you have a Gemini sun (mutable), then one of your survival mechanisms and intrinsic strengths is adaptability. But suppose you're going to be in a situation where you'll need persistence to get your point across? In that case, you may want to do yoga postures for Taurus, a fixed sign known for its endurance and stubbornness, to strengthen your tenacity and opinions so that you don't change your mind in the middle of a negotiation or presentation.

In other words, depending on what you need in a given situation, you can personalize your yoga workout through elements or modalities (or both, if you're really ambitious!) because your intent is key to the process. Remember: in Astro-Yoga, you're using your body as a vehicle for visualization, change, and transformation.

Polarities: Opposites Attract

Another feature of Astro-Yoga involves astrological polarities. A polarity is the sign directly opposite your own. This sign is always in the same modality as yours, in a compatible element, and encompasses qualities that are the opposite of the qualities of your sign. The polarity of Aries, for instance, is Libra. Aries is about independence, while Libra emphasizes cooperation. Aries initiates, and Libra carries through. Aries pioneers, but Libra seeks to balance.

If you're a Libra in need of initiative, willpower, and independence, then you would benefit through the warrior (Aries) series of postures. If you're an Aries who needs some balance and harmony in your life, then the balance (Libra) postures would be beneficial.

The polarity workout is the most accessible because all you have to know is your sun sign. We think of it as the first level of Astro-Yoga. The second level involves using the element and modalities, and the third level is tailored specifically to your natal chart (see Chapter 3 for more on your natal charts). With each level, you're adding layers to your workout, your intent, and your visualization.

Polarities

Cardinal Signs

♈	Aries (fire) independence	♎	Libra (air) cooperation
♋	Cancer (water) nurturing	♑	Capricorn (earth) self-discipline

Fixed Signs

♉	Taurus (earth) stability	♏	Scorpio (water) transformation
♌	Leo (fire) ambition	♒	Aquarius (air) originality

Mutable Signs

♊	Gemini (air) versatility	♐	Sagittarius (fire) idealism
♍	Virgo (earth) detail-oriented	♓	Pisces (water) perfection

When you're doing yoga postures for the polarity of your sun sign, the ease or difficulty of doing the postures or of pulling in the energy related to them often depends on how badly you need the qualities of the opposing sign. An Aries in the throes of a nasty divorce, for example, might find the Libra balance postures difficult to hold for more than a few seconds or feel unwilling to draw on the qualities of Libra during the intent phase of the workout. A Taurus in the same situation might find it difficult to focus on the energetic qualities of Scorpio.

The polarity postures, however, can also work to your benefit. Take the Aries and her nasty divorce. After struggling through the Libra balance postures during intent, she may realize that her difficulties are primarily the result of her own lack of balance and that she needs to be more cooperative. In other words, the Libra postures triggered a shift in consciousness for her.

This shift in awareness is exactly what the postures—combined with your intent—are supposed to do. This is what it means to use your body as a vehicle of visualization for change and transformation.

The Astro-Wheel

The Astro-Wheel concisely summarizes Astro-Yoga. Notice that the polarities are opposite one another: Libra is located between three and four o'clock, while Aries is directly opposite, between nine and ten o'clock. The wheel includes all twelve signs, their elements, the theme of the sign, the name of the associated series of yoga postures, and the keywords used during intent. As you work with the postures, you'll be able to use the Astro-Wheel as a quick reference.

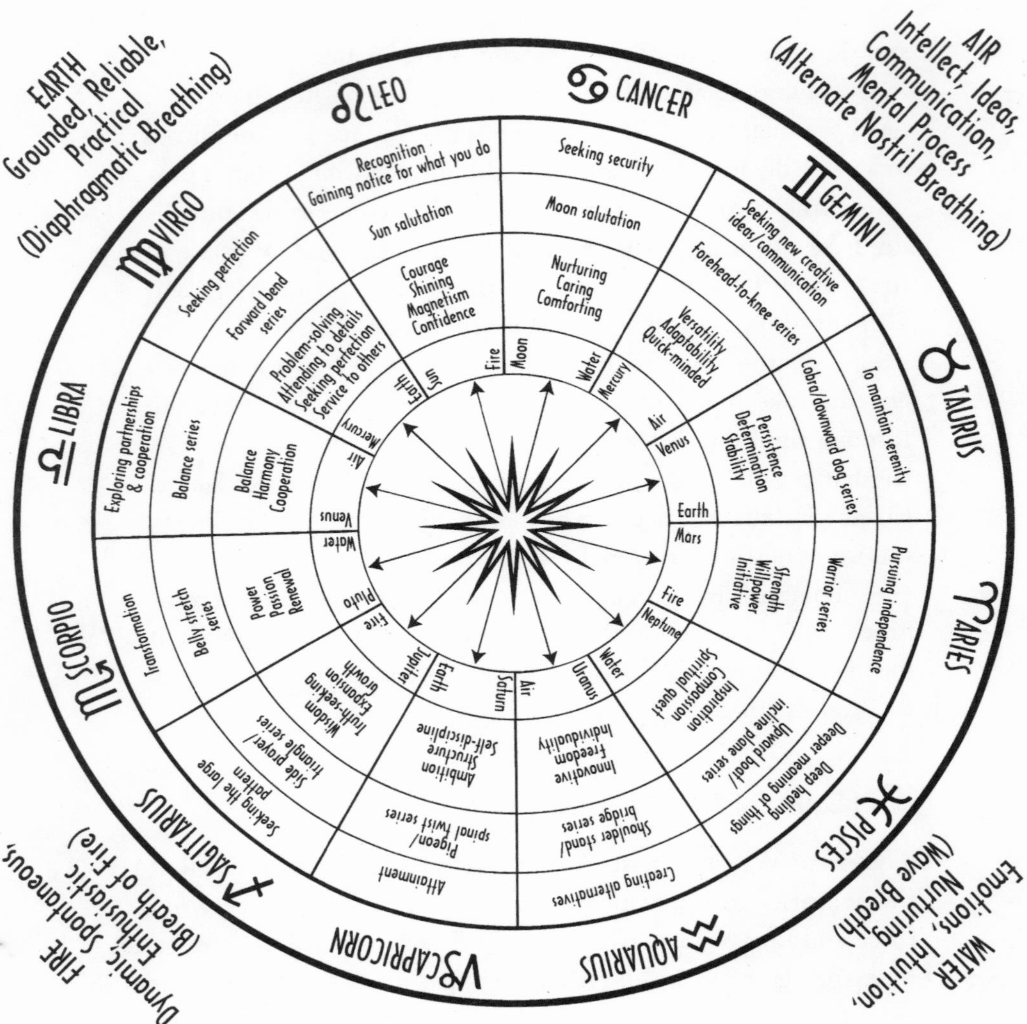

The Astro-Wheel

3

Into the Flow

Try to find a time to practice Astro-Yoga when you won't be distracted by other people. Put the animals in another room. Cats, in particular, are usually happy to join you in yoga, but they don't make good workout companions.

Consistency is important in yoga. Even if you only practice half an hour once or twice a week, it's best to do it at the same time, and on the same day or days of the week. As you get into it, you may find yourself expanding your practice by extending the time and number of workouts per week.

Yoga is best practiced in bare feet and comfortable clothing that is either loose or stretches without binding your body. If the room in which you are working out has a wood, tile, or any other hard surface floor, a yoga mat is recommended. Sticky mats are preferred because your feet won't slip and the mat won't slide along the floor. Some sporting goods stores carry the mats, and they are also available through yoga-oriented catalogues. Ads for the catalogues can be found in *Yoga Journal*, the leading yoga publication.

Warming Up

Before you begin the postures, make sure you spend a few minutes warming up. How you do it—standing up or lying down—is up to you. If you already have a warm-up routine that you've learned in yoga classes or elsewhere, you don't need to read any further.

In Rob's classes, he usually begins with five to ten minutes of easy warm-up stretches combined with focused breathing. Here's how it goes.

Lie on your back, preferably on a yoga mat or carpeting. Take in several deep breaths, inhaling through your nose while pushing your belly out. Exhale, letting your belly sink down toward the spine. Diaphragmatic breathing, as it is known, is a simple breathing exercise, yet considerably different from normal shallow chest breathing.

As you inhale using this method, your abdomen expands and the diaphragm sinks down, massaging the abdominal organs. When you exhale, your abdomen contracts, your diaphragm rises and massages your heart. Your lungs expand to several times the capacity they use during shallow chest breathing, when only the tops of the lungs are used. As a result, more fresh oxygen comes into the cells and more stale carbon dioxide is removed from the body. Your lungs are strengthened as they become more elastic and more air sacs are used.

Feel your neck, shoulders, and back relaxing as you exhale. Stay focused on your breathing. Sense both your body and mind relaxing. You might imagine your breath like a stream of white light coming into your nostrils, flowing into your lungs, and out again. After several deep breaths, slow your breathing, and move the focus of your breath from the diaphragm to the nostrils. Continue this gentle nostril breathing as you move into your stretches.

Now bend your knees, placing your feet flat on the floor. Swing your knees from side to side several times. Raise your knees up again to the starting position. Next, let your knees drop out to the sides as you press the soles of your feet together. Feel the stretch on your hip abductor muscles and gently rock your knees from side to side.

After fifteen or twenty seconds, bring your knees back up and cross your right ankle over your left knee. Drop your head back. Push your tailbone toward the floor. Bring your chin toward your chest, extending your spine. Hold for three or four breaths. Switch legs and repeat.

Straighten your legs. Now we move to the upper body to stretch the shoulders and neck. Still lying down, clasp your hands over your elbows and swing your arms gently from side to side. After several slow repetitions, drop your head to the left as your arms go to the right. Hold for fifteen seconds, stretching your shoulder and neck. Switch sides.

While you're still clasping your elbows, bring your arms back to center above your chest. Inhale and stretch your elbows over your head, toward the floor. As you exhale, swing your arms slowly down along the right side of your body, across your belly, then up along the left side as you inhale again. Repeat the circular movement twice more. Then reverse directions.

As you bring your arms overhead at the end of the last repetition, release your elbows. Clasp your hands together and straighten your arms above the crown of your head and parallel to the floor. Point your index fingers, with the fingertips touching. Now reach for an imaginary object, stretching the upper body. Exhale. Take in another breath and point your toes. Now stretch through your fingertips and toes, lengthening your entire body. Exhale.

Drop your left arm out from the shoulder, turn your head to the left, then, with your right arm still overhead, inhale and stretch through your right hand and right foot, feeling the stretch all along the right side of your body, from your fingertips to your toes. Exhale. Then repeat on the left side.

Next, bend both knees, pick your feet up off the floor, and clasp your hands under your thighs. Rock forward and back and come into a seated position for some neck stretches. As you sit cross-legged, drop your chin to your chest, letting the weight of the head stretch the back of the neck. Raise the head and push your chin toward the ceiling. Repeat the movements, up and down, three or four times. Come back to center and drop your right ear toward your right shoulder, then drop the left ear to your left shoulder. Repeat a few times.

Next, drop your chin to your chest again, but this time rotate your head in a circle, right ear toward right shoulder, head back, then left ear to left shoulder, and chin to chest. Repeat twice, then reverse directions.

After you've finished the neck stretches, remain seated and squeeze your shoulders tightly toward your ears a few times. Then, relaxing your shoulders, place your fingertips on your shoulders and make big circles with your elbows. After several revolutions, reverse directions.

Now rock back and forth and come up to a standing position. Double forward at the waist, letting yourself hang, relaxing your neck, shoulders, and back. Keep your knees soft, not locked. After a few seconds, slowly round up, staying relaxed. Slowly raise your arms up, arch your back, opening the chest. Then gently double forward again. Keep your body limp, and your knees soft. Repeat the Willow Tree, as this warm-up is called, three or four times.

Then hang again. Bend your knees more and take hold of your ankles, folding your belly against your thighs. See if you can wrap your forearms around the back of your calves. If not, keep your arms to the sides of your legs. Now straighten your legs, pulling on your ankles and pushing up through your tailbone as you fold down.

Next, bend your knees and clasp your big toes with your first two fingers. Straighten your legs as best you can, and stretch down. Try to move your shoulders away from your ears, broadening your back. Finally, release your toes and slowly round up to a standing position. Now you've completed your warm-up stretches and you're ready to begin with *form*, focusing on the postures themselves.

Form

With each series, start by simply practicing the postures as described in the following chapters. This process is called *form*. As your body becomes familiar with the postures, they will become easier. Don't be concerned if you aren't able to do the advanced versions of the postures. As you progress in your practice, you'll find that postures which once seemed difficult or impossible become routine parts of the workout.

For example, when Rob was first introduced to a balance posture called the extended-leg squat, he found it extremely difficult. He could only extend a leg while in a deep squat, with his palms pressed together at his chest, for a second or two. But he practiced a modified version, with the hands on the floor by his feet, and in a couple of weeks he was able to easily move into the extended-leg squat with his palms at his chest.

In some schools of yoga, the postures are held for a minute or two, or even longer. Endurance and stamina are required. Usually there are rest periods between the postures. This type of teaching style is known as passive yoga. Astro-Yoga, on the other hand, is a form of active yoga. The postures flow from one to the next, are held for shorter periods of time—usually fifteen to twenty seconds—and use fewer rest periods. However, while you learn the postures, you may want to hold them for at least thirty seconds. This way, your body becomes familiar with the poses and you can work to improve your form.

Notice the ease or difficulty with which you do the postures. Does anything hurt? Which parts of your body feel tight? Do you break into a sweat? Does your heart beat faster? Also notice how you feel emotionally when you do the postures. Does your mood change? Do you feel impatient, happy, irritated, relaxed? Does your mind wander? Are you bored? Stimulated? Indifferent? Our emotions are unusually powerful indicators of *what's really going on*, so if you feel mostly negative while you're doing the postures, explore the possible reasons why.

If you have done yoga for some time, you may be familiar with many of the postures in Astro-Yoga. At the same time, you'll discover that the practice is significantly different from any yoga class you've taken. Instead of using yoga as a sanctuary to escape the daily world for a time, you are practicing the postures to enhance your life by attracting specific energies related to each series. In other words, you are connecting yoga with the rest of your life through a form of visualization and affirmation. The key to receiving the results you want is *intent*.

Intent

In our daily lives, how many of us actually think about our *intent*? We speak of people who intentionally do things to us or we speak of our own intentions to get A and B done by the end of the day. But the kind of intent you bring to Astro-Yoga involves the conscious application of your will to accomplish a specific goal. The goal in this case is to pull in the energy of the sign associated with the series of postures you're performing.

If, when you do the sun salutation, you open your arms as if to embrace the sun but are actually thinking about everything you have to do before you can drop into bed tonight, then you have no intent. You're merely going through the postures. You'll get a good workout, but you're not using your will. Your thoughts are back at home or the office, fussing with family or career obligations. To get the most from an Astro-Yoga workout, you must also bring your mind, heart, and spirit to the process.

If you aren't sure what this means, then eavesdrop on how young children engage in imaginative play. Race car drivers and dolls aren't just inanimate objects made of plastic and cotton. They are *real*, infused with life. They move and talk, get angry and feel joy. Their dramas are happening *now*. Kids bring their powerful wills and imaginations to any kind of play and this is exactly what you need to bring to an Astro-Yoga workout.

Your intent should never involve harm or injury to another person. Even though the Aries in the throes of a nasty divorce may feel like putting a hex on her spouse, she harms only herself when she uses visualization of any sort to harm someone else. There are actually two parts to the intent phase of Astro-Yoga: an affirmation and a visualization. They are intended to work as partners, one complementing the other.

Intent Affirmation

After you've warmed up and done the form for a series, move on to intent. Begin with an intent affirmation, which focuses on the keywords for the sign. Feel free to personalize your affirmation. Tailor it so that you feel comfortable with what you're saying. Examples of intent affirmations will be included in the chapters on each of the signs.

If you're uncertain about how to create an affirmation, just jot down a simple statement about the quality or qualities you're trying to draw into your life. *I'm now drawing imagination and compassion into my life* (Pisces); or, *I now pull personal magnetism into my life* (Leo). Always phrase your affirmation in present tense.

If you are starting with a definite idea of what you want to achieve, be realistic, but bold. Stretch the possibilities. If you're seeking to advance your career, don't settle for a one-step promotion. Think two steps or a giant step ahead. Or think of a way that you could move beyond what you're doing now and into something new that's more appealing, that's more suited for your interests and skills, or the skills you want to develop.

Intent Visualization

As you repeat this affirmation during the intent phase of your workout, vividly imagine the qualities you're seeking as flowing into you, as if on a liquid beam of light. Direct the beam through the top of your head and then down throughout the rest of your body. You can also direct it upward from the earth so that it enters through the root chakra at the base of the spine. The point is to vividly visualize the qualities *coming into you.*

A visualization often consists of images or scenes that depict your goal. Make it vivid, but keep it simple. Put passion and belief behind it. Make it so real that you can see, hear, taste, smell, and touch the outcome. Make it powerful.

The alchemy of visualization seems mysterious to your left brain, but your right brain eats it up. Your right brain knows this language and knows what to do with it. Visualization works. Numerous books have put forth theories about why it works, but if you need to have it proven, try it first with something not related to Astro-Yoga.

Some years ago, Rob was windsurfing on a lake near our home and lost his wallet. Credit cards, driver's license, money, the works. He returned to the lake to look for it on the shore, but couldn't find it. Instead of panicking, he kept running the same visualization: his wallet was resting on his desk, right in front of him. He didn't worry about *how* this would happen; he simply trusted that it would. *He created a vivid, powerful visualization of the end result that he wanted.*

The next day, a stranger rang the doorbell. He'd been fishing in the same lake where Rob had been windsurfing and had reeled in the wallet, which Rob apparently had forgotten to remove from his pocket. Everything inside was soggy, but nothing was missing. Once you're convinced that visualization works, create a visualization that is vivid and simple and use it as you're doing your affirmation. The more sincere your intent, the greater the benefit you derive from the postures.

When the visualization works the way it's supposed to, you may experience a physical sensation. For some people, it's a rushing sensation that suffuses them from the inside out. For others, it's a sensation of heat. You may feel briefly light-headed or you may feel a tingling in your limbs or the tips of your fingers. For other people, it's a mood change. Your spirits suddenly lift, you feel buoyant, optimistic. Or, as in Rob's case, it was a simple sense of conviction that the seemingly impossible would happen. Since each of us is unique, no two people experience the sensation in exactly the same way. You'll recognize it when it happens.

The fact is that most of us visualize all the time and don't even realize it. When you're job hunting or house hunting, for example, the way you decide which one is right for you is by imagining yourself in that house or that job. In a sense, you pull the energy of the house or the job around you and try it on for size. You're doing basically the same thing here, but you're doing it consciously.

If you're dealing with a particular situation or issue, then visualize the situation improving or the issue being resolved and try to physically feel the qualities of what you're pulling in. It's important to do both steps of the intent part of the postures: an affirmation and visualization. This sends a clear signal to your unconscious that you're claiming the power to change your life.

In one of the incarnations of the TV series "Star Trek", Captain Picard has a wonderful saying that can be applied here: "Make it so." That's what intent is. *Make it so.* This simple but powerful statement signals to your subconscious that you mean business, that you are committed.

Creating a Workout

Part of the fun and uniqueness of Astro-Yoga is building a personalized workout that's geared to your particular needs. The system's flexibility makes it possible to alter your workout as your needs change. The brainstorming sections in Chapters 4, 8, 12, and 16, which cover the four elements, are important to that process, so be specific and stick to the issues and situations that you indicate. If you do that for each element, and keep in mind how the modalities work within each element (Chapter 2), you'll be able to design an Astro-Yoga workout that pulls in the energy you need to achieve your goals, whatever they are.

In Rob's workouts, he usually does four signs, one for each element, and typically they are two sets of polar opposites. That is sufficient for a general workout. Over three classes, all twelve series of postures are explored. As you become familiar with the postures in a particular series, you might want to work with variations in the intent phase so that you aren't making an exact duplication of what you did in the form phase.

The brainstorming lists are vital to building your personal workout. They will give you the foundation for creating workouts and allow you the flexibility to change your workout as your needs and goals change. As you examine the lists, ask yourself:

What situations am I facing which require more of this energy? If, after going through the lists, you have more than four signs with check marks, it may be necessary to go through the lists once more to whittle the signs down to four, the ideal number for an hour workout.

When you're doing the brainstorming activities in Chapters 4, 8, 12, and 16, also refer to Appendix A for information on the areas each sign governs.

Levels of Astro-Yoga

In the first level of Astro-Yoga, you are working with your sun sign and its polarity. The second level, which involves the checklists, focuses on the particular qualities related to the various signs and their elements and modalities. In the third, the most personalized level of Astro-Yoga, your birth chart is used as a blueprint for designing your workout. Your birth, or natal, chart describes the energy you may be lacking in your life, which the various postures, coupled with intent, can provide.

A chart is based on your date, place, and exact time of birth. The exact time is vital for accuracy because it determines the sign that was rising at your birth. The rising sign sets up the rest of the chart, which is divided into twelve "houses" that look like wedges in a pie. The sun, moon, and other planets then fall in the various houses, according to their sign and degree.

Charles, whose chart follows, is what astrologers call a triple earth sign. His sun (☉) and rising (the horizontal line that runs through the middle of the chart) are in fixed Taurus, his moon (☽) is in mutable Virgo. In the upper left-hand corner of the chart are graphs that depict the breakdown of his planets by elements and modalities. Notice that he has only one planet in a water sign, four in fire, two in earth, and three in air. However, since his rising is also in earth, let's put the earth breakdown at three. That means that his weakest element is water. Next to the elemental graph is one for modalities. Charles is weakest in cardinal signs.

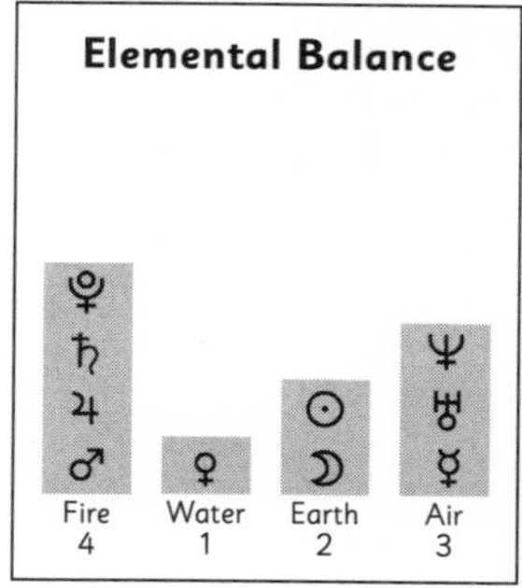

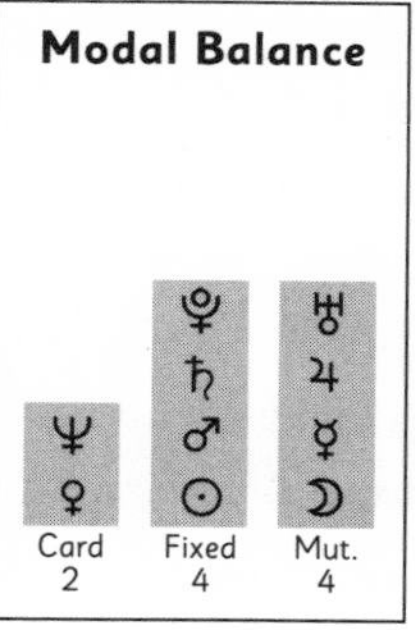

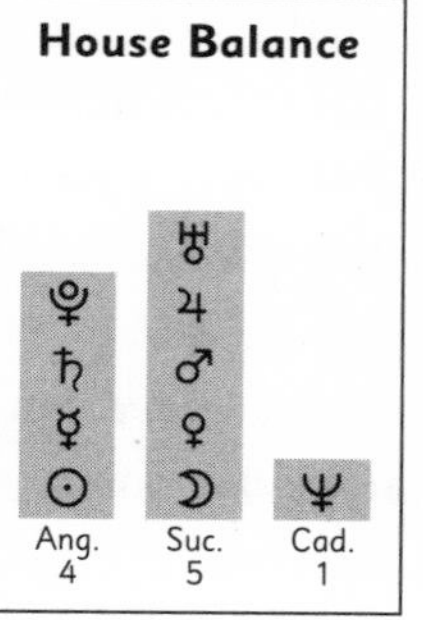

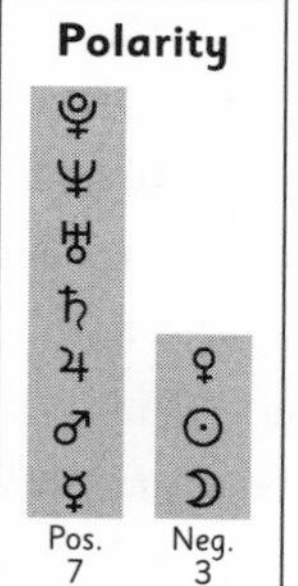

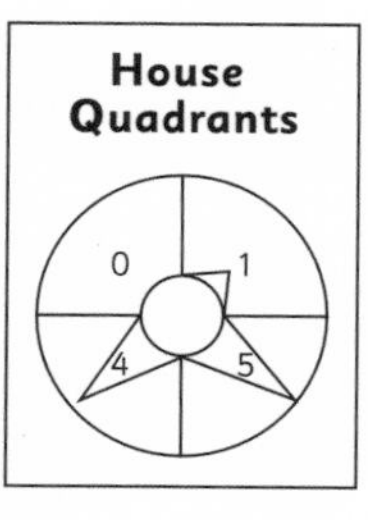

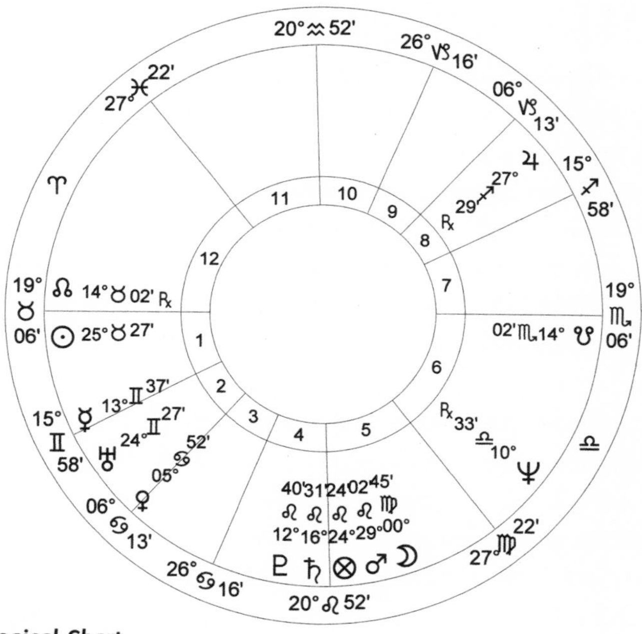

Astrological Chart

Overall, then, Charles benefits from workouts that emphasize water (Cancer, Scorpio, Pisces) and postures related to cardinal energy. Of the cardinal signs, Libra (air), Cancer (water), and Capricorn (earth) are the best for him. He should avoid Aries, however, as it's a fire sign and he already has plenty of fire in his chart. The exception to this is when he's working on particular situations or issues in his life where an abundance of fire is an advantage. Also, he can certainly do the warrior series related to Aries for the physical workout, without using intent. The polarity of Taurus is Scorpio (water), so Charles should include Scorpio postures in his regular workout as well.

When we personalize a workout, we look at the natal chart as a kind of living hologram of the person, a blueprint of potentials. Where is the chart strong or weak? How does the person use energy? What kind of energy does he or she lack?

For example, Diane, a Capricorn, had no planets in water in her chart. The majority of her planets were in fixed signs. When designing a workout for her, we determined that, overall, she needed water sign postures (Cancer, Scorpio, and Pisces) to counterbalance that lack of water in her chart, and either cardinal or mutable sign postures to counterbalance all the fixed planets. In other words, she needed to pull in emotion and intuition (water), focus (cardinal), and flexibility (mutable).

Rob and Trish's daughter has no natal planets in fire signs, so she naturally benefits from fire sign postures, which help to compensate for the lack of this element in her chart. Since she's a double Virgo (sun and moon), it's particularly important for her to do postures for her own sign. Since Pisces is the polarity of Virgo, that's part of her yoga workout too.

Since her chart has a predominance of cardinal planets and only one fixed planet, it's important for her to do postures associated with the fixed signs: Taurus, Leo, Scorpio, and Aquarius. This helps her to persevere in whatever she undertakes.

Even if you don't have your natal chart, you can still benefit from Astro-Yoga. But if you decide it would be helpful, most New Age bookstores offer a computerized natal chart, with the breakdown of elements and modalities (but without an interpretation), for about $5.

Breathing Exercises

Breathing is, of course, vital to life. Without it you would not live very long. Likewise, in yoga, breathing exercises and continual awareness of how you breathe are important aspects of the practice. The breath, like intent, carries prana—the energetic life force—into our bodies. It's also the invisible process that connects the body, mind, and soul.

Breathing exercises also make the lung tissue more elastic while allowing the lungs to expand to a much greater extent by using air sacs that would normally remain idle. Conditions such as allergies, hay fever, and asthma cause tightening of the small bronchi within the lungs. Regular practice of breathing exercises, supplemented by traditional health treatments, has been shown in laboratory experiments to help alter such conditions. By focusing on your breathing, you can release tension as well as constrictions in the lungs, thereby accelerating the healing process. Studies have also shown that the practice of yoga breathing exercises not only improves pulmonary lung function in healthy adults, but may also help reduce the prevalence of bronchial asthma, chronic pulmonary disease, and lung cancer (see Appendix C).

In Astro-Yoga, we include four breathing exercises, one for each element. For example, the Breath of Fire is related to Leo, Sagittarius, and Aries. The description of the breathing exercises can be found at the end of the chapters that focus on the four elements: Chapter 4, fire; Chapter 8, earth; Chapter 12, air; and Chapter 16, water.

Fire

4

Fire: Energy and Action

In Jean Auel's classic book, *Cave of the Clan Bear*, there's a moving scene in which the main characters discover how to create the first spark of fire. If that discovery had not occurred, humanity might never have left the caves. We wouldn't have the luxury of cooked food, hot water, or fuel, and would still be swaddled in animal skins to stay warm.

Fire is yang, primary. It symbolizes life, the force of the spirit, and creative expression. It is dynamic, spontaneous, action-oriented, the thrust that impels us, the will to be. If you've ever seen a forest fire, or watched a TV coverage of one, you were surely struck by its sheer power, its insatiable hunger to consume, and its utter disregard for everything in its path. Intoxicated with its own ubiquity, it sweeps across the earth with the swiftness of thought and, at times, seems to be possessed of consciousness.

By the same token, there is nothing more comforting than a fireplace when you come in out of the cold, a bowl of hot soup when you don't feel up to par, or steaming coffee in the morning. These two extremes typify fire signs.

Fire sign people tend to be aggressive, quick-tempered, and have definite opinions about almost everything. They are leaders who embrace, relish, and revel in experience. For them, life is high drama that involves sweeping passions and big themes. They're the Scarlett O'Haras of the zodiac; initiators and creators; the life of any party. Their enthusiasm and zeal are always infectious. They think on their feet, make snap decisions straight from the gut, and are rarely afraid to take risks.

The shadow side of fire signs is as layered and complex as their more positive attributes. They can be braggarts who don't know when the party is over and it's time to go home. They often believe that their passions are yours, and are hurt or offended when they discover otherwise. Tact and balance are as foreign to them as English is to a native of Nepal. Their impatience may drive you straight up the proverbial wall and their insistence on doing things their way gets tedious very quickly. But in the end, it's easy to forgive their foibles because their zeal and genuine zest for life is so completely refreshing.

When you seek to pull the element of fire into your life, it's necessary to be clear about your *intent*. To clarify what you intend, you have to ask yourself several important questions. What, exactly, are you hoping to bring into your life? Courage? Innovation? New ideas? Magnetism? Truth? The qualities you're seeking usually relate to particular situations or issues in your life. Do you know what those situations or issues are?

Maybe you're trying to break free from a negative relationship or a dead-end job and need the courage to do it. Perhaps you're seeking to integrate the various components of your life but don't know where to begin. One young woman, a Virgo, was in a marriage that no longer worked. She knew she had to leave her husband, but was terrified of taking steps to do so, because she didn't have any real job skills that would enable her to make it as a single mother. Like the lion in the *Wizard of Oz*, she was in desperate need of courage.

She called on the energy of the fire postures, and with time, changed her beliefs about herself and gained the confidence to go back to school to learn a skill. Two years later, she found the courage to end her marriage and begin a new life.

Unless you identify the challenge or the problem in your life and what it is you're hoping to create in the future, your intent won't be clear. If your intent isn't clear, you won't receive the maximum benefits of Astro-Yoga.

In the following exercise, there's a space for you to write out situations or issues in your life that you would like to work on. Keep it simple and clear. Maybe the issue is getting a promotion. Maybe it's finding a new direction for your life or improving a relationship.

Once this is done, you then have to ask yourself what attributes you will need. Glance through the lists on page 38 with this question in mind, and check only the attributes that apply to your situation.

Using the Lists

When you glance over these lists, your first reaction will probably be: who wouldn't want to gain all those attributes? The answer is simple—the people who already have them.

If you look at the lists in terms of who you are now, and if you're really honest with yourself, you'll find that you already possess some of these attributes. It may be that your spiritual values are utterly clear to you, but that you're a bit low in the pride department when it comes to your work. Does the situation or issue you jotted in the top line pertain to work? If it does, then that's where you begin to apply the energy you pull in through the various fire postures. Make sure that in the last section of the exercise you have checked "work"—or the appropriate area.

The section that has the most check marks signifies the fire sign energy that you need most to address the situation or issue at hand. If no area has more checks than any other, you can then select any of the series of postures related to the three fire signs.

Brainstorming

Fire Sign Attributes

The situations or issues that I would like to work on are: ____________

____

Aries Attributes

Action ____________ Initiative ____________

Assertiveness ____________ Innovation ____________

Enthusiasm ____________ New ideas ____________

Independence ____________ Risk ____________

Leo Attributes

Confidence ____________ Optimism ____________

Courage ____________ Personal integrity ____________

Honor ____________ Pride ____________

Nobility ____________ Strength ____________

Sagittarius Attributes

Big picture ____________ Illumination ____________

Blunt honesty ____________ Spiritual path/values ____________

Expansion ____________ Truth ____________

Growth ____________ Wisdom ____________

Areas of my life which pertain to situation or issue

Finances ____________ Spirituality ____________

Personal relationships ____________ Work/profession ____________

General self-improvement ____________

Other notes to myself:

____

____

____

____

____

____

Your Body and Fire Signs

In astrology, each sign governs a particular part of the body, which is considered to be the most vulnerable area for that sign.

In designing your workout, it's a good idea to include postures related to the parts of the body your sun sign rules. Sagittarius, for instance, rules the hips, thighs, muscles, sciatic nerves, and motor nerve action. So if you're a Sagittarian, you should pay extra attention to the side prayer and triangle postures, which open the hips and stretch the thigh muscles as well as the back. The following table lists the fire signs and the parts of the body they rule.

Parts of the Body Ruled by Fire Signs

Fire Sign	Part of Body
♈ *Aries, cardinal*	*Head, face, brain, eyes*
♌ *Leo, fixed*	*Heart, upper back, sides*
♐ *Sagittarius, mutable*	*Hips, thighs, muscles, sciatic nerves, and motor nerve action*

What's Coming Up

In the next three chapters, we'll be talking about the individual fire signs and illustrating the Astro-Yoga postures that go with each one. Then we'll move on to the other elements and their signs. Before you start, glance once more at the brainstorming checklist to see which attributes you've checked under each sign. If one sign has more checks than any of the others, read that sign first, then try the yoga postures.

After you've done the postures the first time, try them again with *intent*. Theoretically, most of us understand what intent is. But in a practical sense, it varies from person to person. Be specific: *I'm now pulling in courage and magnetism.*

The Breath of Fire

You can bolster your intent for the fire signs by doing the energetic breathing exercise, known as the Breath of Fire, either before or after you do a series of postures for one of the fire signs. Here's how.

Begin in a seated position with your legs crossed. Take in a deep breath, then forcefully expel the air through your nose as you pull in your belly. As you breathe in again, let your belly go out naturally without forcing it, then exhale again pulling in the belly.

As you continue on, remember that the emphasis is on the exhalation. If you're not sure that you are doing it right, just imagine that a small bug has flown into your nostril and you expel it with a forceful exhalation through the nose. With practice, you can pick up speed. Try doing two sets, each for about thirty seconds. Before beginning the second set, focus on the energy of the sign as you did in the postures. Say the keywords to yourself, then begin the breathing exercise.

5

Aries, the Ram

Theme:
Independence
Keywords:
Initiative, willpower, strength, leadership, pioneering
March 21–April 19
Ruled by Mars
Cardinal fire
Rules head, face, brain

Mars, son of Jupiter and Juno, was the god of war, known for his savagery, violence, and love of bloodshed. That's hardly a rave review for the planet that rules this sign, but it captures the Aries drive and energy.

Male or female, the Aries individual is bold, brash, and utterly fearless. His endless reserves of energy keep him on the move constantly, whether it's to drive his son's Little League team to games or to pioneer new projects where he works. Thank Mars, his ruling planet, for all that energy.

His leadership abilities are obvious to everyone and were probably apparent from a young age. He was the kid who set up the lemonade stand in your neighborhood, then got the other kids to work for him. This same type of spirit characterizes everything he does. He's an initiator, the person who comes up with ideas and launches them.

Unless his interest and passion are sustained, however, he may have trouble finishing what he starts. This is usually more of a problem for other people than it is for him, since he probably doesn't perceive it as a problem to begin with. It can create havoc in the lives of other people, however, who are depending on him to fulfill a responsibility or obligation. Even if he lacks persistence, he compensates for it by sheer drive and ambition.

He's an excellent executive, aggressive and competitive. He relies on his own judgment and intuition to make decisions. Even if he has failed at endeavors in the past, he exudes a successful image in spite of it. His unshakable confidence in himself, in fact, is one of his greatest strengths. When confronted with the possibility of attempting something he has never done before, whether it's rock climbing or running for political office, he doesn't even question *if* he can do it. He knows he can.

His temper is probably legendary, as he finds it difficult to bite his tongue when his sensibilities are offended. He's argumentative by nature, and this doesn't help matters. But the good news is that once he blows, that's it. He rarely holds a grudge. Even if the other person remembers the incident clearly, it passes out of the Aries awareness almost as soon as the explosion is over.

Some of his enormous energy goes into sports—either sports that he plays or in which he participates vicariously through his children and friends. The more daring Aries individuals enjoy thrill sports like auto racing and rough-and-tumble sports like football. But every Aries needs some sort of activity which can burn off energy.

Boldness, independence, impatience: all these adjectives fit him, but they're hardly the full picture. While his dynamic energy and lack of subtlety and nuance may intimidate loved ones and strangers alike, they admire the way he tackles obstacles with a single-minded purpose that would bring less aggressive individuals to their knees.

The problem is that he often plows ahead without regard for other people. There's an element of selfishness to Aries that you shouldn't hold against him. The "me first" part of his personality is simply how he defines himself in the world. It allows him to forge ahead, taking risks the rest of us wouldn't even contemplate. If the people around him can't move at his pace, he leaves them gasping in the dust.

Aries is a pioneer, a trailblazer, the kind of individual who forges new paths for the rest of us. His pioneering spirit is similar to the early settlers who ventured across America in wagon trains. It's the same energy that eventually will colonize space. There's no stopping him when he gets an idea that ignites his passions. He enjoys being in charge and his enthusiasm and passion ignite others. He literally brims with innovative ideas and wants them all put into effect yesterday. As a result, he may take on more than he can actually handle, and if he doesn't learn to delegate, burnout is a real possibility.

The challenge for Aries is to sustain his interest so that he finishes what he starts. He won't see it this way, of course, because he's so accustomed to walking away without regret or guilt. He's used to not looking back. There's nothing inherently wrong with this and it may be one of his survival mechanisms to avoid burnout. But if he can develop more balance in his life, he might not take on so much to begin with.

Building a Personalized Workout

Most Aries individuals need balance in their lives. So if you're reading this chapter because you're an Aries, then glance through the Libra section and try out the Libra balance postures. You may want to include these in your personalized workout.

If you're reading this chapter because your brainstorming list puts you squarely in need of some Aries energy, then read through the warrior postures. Your first time through these postures should be to familiarize yourself with the series. Your second time through the postures should be done with intent.

Intent affirmation: *I now pull in initiative, leadership, willpower, innovation, new ideas, and independence.*

Alter your affirmation to fit your needs. Maybe you need initiative and leadership abilities rather than independence. If so, then your affirmation might be: *I now pull in initiative and leadership abilities.*

Intent visualization: As you repeat this affirmation during the intent phase of your workout, vividly imagine the qualities you're seeking as flowing into you. You might see yourself as a warrior in armor with a shield and a sword, or you might see yourself accompanied by such a warrior as you call on the energy of Aries. As you do so, you might visualize yourself in a particular situation in which you need the energy of your warrior guide.

After you do the warrior series, you'll feel physically and spiritually energized. To maintain the Aries energy, you may want to repeat the affirmation several times before you enter a situation in which you need those qualities, or even as you're falling asleep at night. This process helps to make your intent utterly clear to your unconscious.

Jim, a Cancer, was applying for a small-business loan to expand his bookstore. He did the warrior series for several days before he went into the bank to apply for the loan and did them again the morning of his meeting at the bank.

Each time, as he practiced the postures with intent, he imagined the end result of the loan—an expanded store with double the stock he currently carried and triple the customers. He saw the inside of the store in vivid detail—a small coffee shop, the new equipment he needed, and the addition he planned to build. Instead of seeing his store in cutthroat competition with the bigger chain bookstores, he imagined *abundance* for his business. He did his visualization without the thought of harming or depriving anyone else, and he got his loan.

The Warrior Series

No matter what your sign is, when you perform the Aries postures, you pull in assertiveness, independence, willpower, leadership abilities, and the knack to initiate new projects. You are drawing on the power of Mars, which can provide energy to manifest what you desire.

The Aries series, based on the warrior postures, are strong, energetic, and repeated several times with variations, but they are only held for ten to fifteen seconds. Aries energy is about entering new territory, taking action, initiating; it's not about endurance or persistence.

Before you begin the postures, make sure you spend a few minutes warming up. Once you're ready, you begin with *form*, focusing on the postures and how your body reacts to them. The warrior postures strengthen the legs, hips, back, arms, and shoulders. They expand the chest and improve your stamina.

After you've gone through the postures, you move on to *intent*. Bring to mind what you want to achieve. Focus on your intent. Keep the keywords in mind. Visualize the end result. Bring emotion and passion into your effort.

The Mountain

Start in the **mountain** pose, the yoga standing posture. If you are using a yoga mat or towel, stand at the back of the mat. Your feet are close together. Your back is straight, your shoulders relaxed, your chest forward, and your knees soft, rather than locked. Close your eyes. Pay attention to your breath for about thirty seconds. This relaxed pose will allow you to center yourself and let go of everything that you were thinking about before you started. Now you're ready to move into the Aries warrior postures.

Warrior One

Take a giant step forward with your right leg and plant your foot firmly down. Turn your left heel in about thirty degrees. Keep the left leg straight, bend your right knee. Ideally, your right thigh will form a ninety-degree angle with the lower leg so that the thigh is parallel with the floor. But don't force the posture, especially if you're not accustomed to doing warrior postures or if you're not particularly flexible. With Astro-Yoga, the clarity of your intent is primary; the perfection of the posture comes in its own time. Know how to do the posture, but don't obsess about it.

As you bend your knee, raise your arms up overhead. Work at bringing your shoulders back with your arms close to your ears. If possible, push your knee further forward and your hips further down. Look straight ahead. As you repeat the posture during the series, you can extend the stretch by looking up (Figure 5-1). Keep your arms as straight as you can with the palms facing each other and your hips facing forward. If you want to go deeper into the posture, sink your hips down an inch or two further, look up toward your thumbs, and give your back a slight arch.

Breathe. Don't hold your breath. In Astro-Yoga, prana—the cosmic force that the body takes in as we breathe—engages the sun sign's energy, pulling its influences into the body. If you're working on intent, reach for the Aries energy. Think *leadership*.

Hold the posture for three breaths, then lower your arms and step back with your right foot, assuming the mountain pose again. Take a couple of slow breaths, then another giant step forward, this time with the left foot, and assume warrior one on this side.

Step back. Now bend over and hang with your shoulders relaxed for several seconds as you incorporate the new energy into your being. Then slowly round up, coming up one vertebra at a time.

Warrior Two

Step forward with the right leg and repeat warrior one, making sure that your left heel is turned in. This time, while you are still in the full expression of the posture, turn your hips and upper body to the side. Lower your right arm to shoulder level and extend your left arm behind you at the same level. Now look over your right shoulder toward your fingertips as you enter the **warrior two** posture (Figure 5-2). Reach for the energy. Think *initiative*. Return to warrior one, hold, then step back.

Now go into warrior one from the left side, then move into warrior two. As you progress through the postures, you repeat each one, creating a flow of energy. As you hold the postures during the intent phase, think about your goal, if you are working with one, and concentrate on pulling in energy. Imagine threads

Figure 5-1
Warrior
One

Figure 5-2
Warrior
Two

of energy entering your fingertips, running down your arms, and filling your body with positive energy.

Fierce Warrior

As you come back into the mountain posture, fold down again. This time, after you've rolled down, bend your knees and sink toward a half-squat, then reach up, raising your torso upright. Extend your arms upward and look up at your thumbs as you assume the **fierce warrior** posture (Figure 5-3). Think *willpower*. This posture, in particular, strengthens your legs and hips and builds stamina. Hold for three breaths, then stand up, reaching overhead for one long breath, and lower your arms.

Warrior Two Reversed

Step forward with your right leg and assume warrior one. Hold for at least fifteen seconds, then flow into warrior two. After three breaths, turn your right palm up and reach overhead as you lower your left hand to your thigh in **warrior two reversed** (Figure 5-4). If you want to go further, slide your left hand down your leg toward your calf and bend your forward knee further. Think *independence*. Come back up into warrior two, shift to warrior one, then step back and lower your arms.

Repeat the postures on the opposite side by stepping forward with your left leg. Remember to pull in the energy as you go through each variation during the intent phase. Think or say out loud a different term associated with Aries—leadership, initiative, independence, taking risks—each time you pull in the energy. Keep in mind that Astro-Yoga is not a rigid discipline. Any of the keywords can be applied to any of the postures within the series. But you may find that certain keywords seem to fit particular poses especially well.

As you complete the second side and come back to the mountain posture, fold down again. Hang and relax for ten seconds. Then bend your thighs into your chest and extend your arms out to the sides as you raise them overhead. Look up with hands in the fierce warrior pose. Think *taking risks*. Again, feel

Figure 5-3 Fierce Warrior

Figure 5-4 Warrior Two Reversed

the energy passing through your body. Stand up and return to the mountain.

As you finish your last posture, relax into the mountain for at least ten seconds. Don't obsess about the time. Do what feels comfortable for you. Trust your body's wisdom; it knows how long to hold a pose.

Variations

There is no stringent formula for postures in any of the series. You can work in variations. If you find warrior one too strenuous, for instance, you might try the **kneeling warrior** (Figure 5-5). In this posture, you step forward as before, but drop down to your

Figure 5-5 Kneeling Warrior

Figure 5-6 Warrior Three

knee with your back leg. Raise both arms and look up toward your thumbs as you push your hips down and forward. Pull in the Aries energy saying one of the keywords.

After you've gotten familiar with the warrior postures and are confident in your practice, you might try the postures by starting at the front of your mat and stepping back into a lunge with your hands down on either side of your forward foot (see the extended-leg lunge in Chapter 6, Figure 6-8). From that position, you can raise up into warrior one. This method allows you to go deeper into your posture, especially if your back foot is raised up on your toes.

You can also add the **warrior three** posture as a variation. In this posture, you start in the lunge position and raise your arms in front of you. Then, you lean forward and lift the back leg up as you come into balance on your front foot (Figure 5-6).

Breath of Fire

Once you've completed the series, you can move on to the Breath of Fire. See Chapter 4 for details.

6

Leo, the Lion

Theme:
Recognition—gaining notice for what you do
Keywords:
Courage, confidence, shining, magnetism
July 23–August 22
Ruled by the sun
Fixed fire
Rules heart, back, spine, wrists

If there's ever any doubt about the intrinsic energy of Leo, tune in to a Discovery Channel special about lions in the wild. Watch them hunt, care for their young, and snuggle up to their mates. Everything the lion does is characterized by expressiveness, confidence, nobility, and strength.

This is the energy you want to pull in if you need to shine in some area of your life. Even when you don't feel very self-confident, Leo's energy will make it seem that confidence is your middle name. If you're depressed, Leo's energy will bolster your spirits. If you're unemployed or looking for a new job, this energy will take you where you need to be.

The Leo individual has an innate sense of drama, and life is certainly her stage. Her flamboyance and magnetism show up in dozens of ways, from the clothes she wears to the car she drives and the ways she relates to others. No one could ask for a more loyal and compassionate friend, but in return she expects her friends to believe as she does, and to be interested in what interests her. When they're not, she takes it personally, and her feelings get hurt.

This propensity of hers stems from a deep need for recognition and acknowledgment from others. The recognition doesn't have to come from the larger world, although that would be just fine, but she needs it most from the people in *her* world. In fact, the one sure way that others can coerce her is to withhold their approval and recognition.

She has a tremendous need for self-expression and, in some form or another, it emerges as a dominant theme in her life. It's no wonder that Leos rule theater and the allied arts. Numerous actors and actresses have Leo prominent in their charts—as sun, moons, or rising signs. Probably the most famous Leo woman in recent times was Jackie Onassis, who typified the archetype. Her leonine mane of hair, her brilliant smile, and her dignity are all Leo traits. Even though Onassis never sought the spotlight, which made her atypical of most Leos, it was where she ended up.

The typical Leo is warm, outgoing, and fun, with an essentially optimistic nature. Kids gravitate toward her because they sense a kindred soul. She thinks nothing of getting down and dirty and rolling around on the floor with a three-year-old. A therapist might refer to this as being in touch with her inner child, but for her, it's business as usual.

Leos are often accused of having inflated egos. This may be how it appears, but the truth is that she often feels insecure, not quite up to snuff, so she tries to cover it up with flamboyance. The irony, though, is that her magnetism is genuine. It's as if she were born with a quality that the rest of us spend our entire lives seeking to cultivate. And it's this magnetism that helps her achieve whatever she sets her sights on.

Her emotions are often as dramatic and bold as the clothes she wears. When her passions are really at their peak, she's like director James Cameron the night he won the Oscar for *Titanic* —on top of the world, king of the universe. When her emotions plunge her into despair, she doesn't stay there very long because, well, ultimately it's pretty boring. Besides, her optimism won't stand for it and usually rescues her quickly.

These same passions make her an ardent lover and romantic and, once she's bitten, she falls hard and commits fully. This is as true of her relationships as it is of her dreams. If she has some childhood dream that she hopes to fulfill, her fixed and persistent nature helps her to achieve it and, perhaps, to achieve it beyond anything she has imagined.

The challenge for Leo is actually fairly simple: don't take everything so personally. Just because her significant other doesn't believe the same things she does or have exactly the same interests, she shouldn't take it as a personal slight. She must learn to accept the diversity in human nature and be a bit more flexible in her approach to herself and others.

Building a Personalized Workout

Think of the Leo/Aquarius polarity as the emperor versus the humanitarian. The emperor rules his kingdom with a big heart and enormous generosity to his subjects—but only as long as his subjects acknowledge that he's the ruler. The humanitarian couldn't care less about personal kingdoms or people paying him homage; his stage is the world and his goal is to make it a better place for everyone.

Most Leos benefit from emotional detachment and learning to honor individuality and diversity, the very areas where Aquarius is strongest. So if you're reading the Leo chapter because you're a Leo, turn to the Aquarius chapter and read through the shoulder stand/bridge series of postures. Consider including them in your personalized workout.

If you're reading the Leo section because your brainstorming list indicates you need Leo energy, then glance through the sun salutation postures. Pay special attention to the postures that "open the heart," the area of the body that Leo rules. Hold these positions longer and focus your intent on them when you do the series. Your first time through the sequence should be to familiarize yourself with the series. Your second time through should be done with *intent*.

Intent affirmation: *I now pull in creative expression, confidence, courage, strength, and nobility.*

Personalize your affirmation to address the specific situations or conditions of your life. If you have enough creative expression at the moment, but would like to have more self-confidence, then your affirmation might be: *I now pull in self-confidence.* Keep it simple and direct. Repeat it often during the intent phase of the workout.

Intent visualization: As you say your Leo affirmation, vividly imagine the qualities you're seeking as flowing into you. You might visualize a roaring lion charging into you as you absorb its energy. Or you might see yourself transformed into the majestic lion.

A 29-year-old Leo woman landed her dream job with a head-hunting firm. Two months into her new career, however, all her doubts began to emerge. Even though she had glowing reports from her boss, she felt she wasn't competent for the job. Her belief in her incompetence quickly brought about careless errors in her work. She was reprimanded several times, which only undermined her already flagging self-confidence.

In designing her Astro-Yoga workout, we recommended that she stick to her own sun sign and make the sun salutation prominent in her workout. We suggested that she also practice the Breath of Fire and focus her intent during these breathing exercises. After several weeks of daily practice, she began to see a turnaround at work and she gained confidence and respect from her boss.

To maintain the Leo energy boost after you've completed the postures with intent, you may want to repeat the affirmation several times before you enter a situation in which you need those qualities, or even as you're falling asleep at night. This helps to make your intent utterly clear to your unconscious.

The depth of your intent usually determines the degree to which you feel the energy in your body. If you're distracted or would rather be doing something else, you probably won't get the maximum benefits of the postures. The point is to be focused when you voice your intent and to remain as focused as possible.

The Sun Salutation

This series is undoubtedly the best-known series of yoga postures and is a mainstay in most schools of yoga. It's a flowing, graceful series of postures, each one counteracting the stretch of the previous one. One pose expands the chest as you inhale, while the next contracts the chest as you exhale. The postures improve flexibility of the spine, stretch the major muscle groups, strengthen the heart, and improve circulation.

If you've taken yoga classes and done the sun salutation, you'll probably find this series familiar, but not identical to the sun salutation that you have done before. However, keep in mind that the use of intent is what distinguishes Astro-Yoga.

Prayer Position

Begin by standing at the front of your mat in the mountain posture with your feet together, back straight, and shoulders relaxed. Look straight ahead. Inhale deeply through your nose, then exhale and bring your palms together at your sternum as you assume the **prayer position** (Figure 6-1).

Standing Back Arch

Inhale and reach up, either looking forward or up toward your thumbs with a slight arch to your back (Figure 6-2). With each repetition of this posture, allow yourself to arch your back slightly more.

Standing Forward Bend

Now bend at the waist, reaching out as far in front of you as you can. Reach down for your feet, folding your upper body toward your thighs. Place your hands on either side of your feet, bending your knees if necessary. Exhale as you go (Figure 6-3).

Bent-Knee Lunge

Stay aware of your breath and step back into a lunge with your right foot. Drop your right knee to the floor. Look up and push your hips down (Figure 6-4).

Figure 6-1 Prayer Position

Figure 6-2 Standing Back Arch

Figure 6-3 Standing Forward Bend

Plane Position

Step back with your left foot and straighten both legs in the **plane position** (Figure 6-5). Keep your legs, back, and neck in a straight line, with your hands placed flat on the floor and close to your body.

Extended-Arm Child's Pose

Now drop to both knees and slide back, bringing your buttocks toward your heels. Press your palms down and push forward to sink further down (Figure 6-6).

Crouching Cat

Slide forward from the extended-arm child's pose, keeping your nose just above the mat. Pause in the **crouching cat** as your head comes between your arms. Your back should be arched with the tailbone up. Make sure your elbows don't flare out to the sides.

Figure 6-4 Bent-Knee Lunge

Figure 6-5 Plane Position

Figure 6-6 Extended-Arm Child's Pose

The Cobra

Inhale and slide forward with your nose and forehead just above your mat and keep your tailbone raised. As your shoulders come over your hands, press your hips and thighs down as you straighten your legs. Simultaneously, press down with your palms and raise your chest and belly, arching your back to come into the **cobra** posture (Figure 6-7). Remember to keep your elbows pressed in toward your rib cage and your shoulders down and back.

Downward-Facing Dog

Raise your hips from the cobra, then push back through your tailbone as you straighten your legs and drop the crown of your head toward the mat (see Figure 9-5). Press your heels down and arch your lower back. While the **downward-facing dog** is part of the sun salutation, the posture is emphasized in the Taurus, rather than Leo, postures.

Extended-Leg Lunge

Lower your hips as you move back into the plane position, again with the legs, back, and neck aligned as you look between your hands. Lift your head and lunge your right foot forward next to your hand (Figure 6-8). If you can't lunge that far, grab your ankle and pull your foot forward into the **extended-leg lunge**. Keep your head up and your left leg straight.

Standing Forward Bend

Now step forward with your left foot in the **standing forward bend** again (Figure 6-9). Stretch down, then open your arms to the side as you come up.

Standing Back Arch

Reach over your head, look up toward your thumbs, and arch your back into the **standing back arch**. Lower your arms and come back into the mountain posture. Repeat the sequence, this time leading with the left leg.

Try three to five rounds. Starting with the second or third round, move from form to intent and begin using the keywords:

Figure 6-7 The Cobra

Figure 6-8 Extended-Leg Lunge

Figure 6-9 Standing Forward Bend

courage, *confidence*, *shining*, and *magnetism* as you go through the postures. You can use one word per posture or, if you are holding the postures for several breaths, you may want to use more than one word. Think of your body as a vehicle for pulling in the fire, specifically the energy of Leo.

The Breath of Fire

Now you can sit down for a couple of rounds of the Breath of Fire, again working with your intent. See Chapter 4 for a description of the breathing exercise.

7

Sagittarius, the Archer

Theme:
Seeking the big picture
Keywords:
Growth, expansion, wisdom, truth-seeking
November 22–December 21
Ruled by Jupiter
Mutable fire
Rules hips, thighs, muscles, sciatic nerves

Remember the story about Diogenes, who lit a candle and roamed through the dark in search of truth? That's Sagittarius. The truth seeker. In his search for the bigger picture, Sagittarius is outspoken, often to the point of bluntness, and sometimes fails to recognize the importance of the smaller picture. It's the reverse of that adage about not being able to see the forest through the trees. He can see the forest just fine; it's the trees that challenge him.

This is the energy to tap if you're puzzled about which direction to go in some area of your life. It won't tell you how to get where you want to be, but it provides the larger picture that enables you to see things as if from a bird's-eye view. Or use this energy if you need to expand your life in some way. Perhaps you want to learn new skills or go back to school. Maybe you want a larger house to accommodate your growing family. Maybe you need a substantial raise. Wherever the expansion is needed, Sagittarian energy will pull it into your life.

Even though Sagittarius, as a fire sign, is action-oriented, he's as mental as Gemini, his polar opposite. Gemini, however, is more concerned about the here and now and is propelled by curiosity; Sagittarius is oriented toward the future and is propelled by his search for the truth.

The underlying theme of his life, in fact, is about expansion and growth. He's not the type who sets specific goals that have to be achieved by a certain date. That's not his style. He's more likely to have some private, idealistic vision that guides him, and if it isn't conscious, it's an inner prompting or urging so strong that he feels he must follow it.

Sagittarians come in two broad types. The first type places a high value on personal freedom—that is, he doesn't like being told what to do or when to do it. This type, especially when younger, is apt to take off for Europe or some far-flung corner of the world on a moment's notice, with nothing more than a backpack and a credit card. He travels to see what lies beyond the shores of his own world. He does so to resist spells of despair or a rapidly encroaching sense of being trapped.

The second type may also travel on a whim, but does it with a deeper purpose in mind—to sample foreign cultures and belief systems, to immerse himself in philosophies and religions that differ from his own. This would include the business traveler or even a soccer mom. What he's really seeking is wisdom. Either type, though, is part of the overall archetype of the sign and merely represents a phase of development.

Some Sagittarians (sun, moon, or rising) might spend their early adult lives traveling in a professional capacity—flight attendants, travel agents, or businesspeople whose jobs take them all over the place. Then, between the ages of thirty-five and forty-two, they may suddenly change professions, and travel becomes secondary to a personal search for the bigger picture. The cosmic Sagittarius then emerges.

Like his fellow fire sign, Leo, the Sagittarian's nature is basically optimistic and friendly. And like his mutable cousins,

Gemini and Pisces, he's adaptable, versatile, and flexible—as long as his personal freedom and idealism aren't impinged upon. Freedom and idealism are the underlying themes of his life and his challenge is to integrate them into who he is and how he lives.

If, for instance, he's in a job or a relationship that restricts his freedom, then he must take positive steps to change his situation—steps that show his intent. In the meantime, to counter the restrictions, he should do at least one thing daily that is strictly for himself. Then he will marvel at how the universe works in cooperation with his intent.

Sagittarians bring their internal quests to Astro-Yoga. That may be said of all the signs, of course, but with this sign, the quest is such a major part of his life that he usually succeeds rapidly in integrating the physical postures with his intent.

The shadow side of Sagittarius involves being "right." When he finds a belief system or philosophy that suits him, he can't understand why everyone else doesn't buy into it, too. This is a trait he shares with his Leo sibling, but with the typical Sagittarius, the motive is quite different. Whereas Leo perceives agreement with her beliefs as proof that you love her, Sagittarius sees his beliefs as correct, and therefore, if they're correct, everyone should hold them. While that may or may not be true, Sagittarius benefits from learning tolerance.

Building a Personalized Workout

The polarity for Sagittarius is Gemini, the communicator, the sign that seeks to fit together the pieces that form the big picture and which is more tolerant of individual differences than Sagittarius. If you're a Sagittarian, then read the Gemini description and the forehead-to-knee series for that sign. Consider including them in your workout.

If you're reading this section because your brainstorming list indicates you need the Sagittarian energy, then read through the postures to acquaint yourself with them. When you do the workout for the first time, notice which postures emphasize the hips, which Sagittarius rules. It might be a good idea to emphasize these postures as you personalize your workout.

Intent affirmation: *I now pull in expansion, spiritual and creative growth, wisdom, and the big picture.*

Personalize your affirmation in whatever way suits you, addressing the specific qualities you would like to bring into your life. If you feel quite expansive in your life at the moment, but are in need of spiritual growth and wisdom, then your affirmation might be: *I now pull spiritual growth and wisdom into my life*. Keep it simple and direct.

Intent visualization: As you repeat this affirmation during the intent phase of your workout, vividly imagine these qualities flowing into you. You might imagine an archer shooting an arrow of light at you, providing you with the energy of Sagittarius. Imagine the arrow filling your body with light. Make the visualization vivid so that you feel the qualities coming into you. Also, make it as specific as possible.

Russ, a 36-year-old Capricorn, had a difficult time coming up with a visualization. He was an attorney who wanted to get out of the rat race and start a bed-and-breakfast with his wife. The problem was that he didn't know which area of the country he wanted to live in and couldn't visualize a B&B without knowing where it would be situated. We advised him to forget the location for the time being, and focus on the building. Sketch it, find photographs of a place that approximated what he wanted, look on the Internet for possible sites.

He found a photo that was pretty close to what he and his wife were looking for and this helped him in his visualization. Within six months, the perfect place came on the market, a B&B in North Carolina that was a nearly perfect match of the facility he visualized.

To maintain the Sagittarian energy boost after you've completed the postures with intent, repeat the affirmation several times before you enter a situation in which you need those qualities, or even as you're falling asleep at night. This helps to make your intent utterly clear to your unconscious.

The depth of your intent usually determines the degree to which you feel the energy in your body. If you're distracted or would rather be doing something else, you probably won't get the maximum benefits of the postures. The point is to be focused when you voice your intent and to remain as focused as possible.

Side Prayer/Triangle Series

Like the other fire signs, the Sagittarius series is energetic and somewhat demanding. The triangle postures, in particular, are a familiar part of most yoga classes. These postures, however, are held for a longer period of time than the *asanas* in the sun salutation. Rather than flowing one into another, they create a fire within, building stamina and endurance. The hips and thighs, which are ruled by Sagittarius, are activated throughout most of the postures. The hamstrings are stretched and the spine becomes supple with the twists that are integral to the postures.

Begin the series in the mountain posture, the standing yoga posture, at the front of your mat. Take several deep breaths, then bend at the waist and let the upper half of your body hang.

Standing Side Prayer

Next, bend your knees and lower your body into a partial squat. With your hand, turn your knees a few inches to the right. Then, twisting your upper torso to the left, bring your right elbow or upper arm to the outside of your left knee. Bring your palms together near your heart; your left elbow should point upward, the right elbow toward the mat (Figure 7-1). Now you're in the **standing side prayer**. If you want to expand the stretch, slide your left arm down so that the armpit comes to the outside of the knee. Hold here for three breaths.

Standing Side Stretch

If you want to try a more advanced pose, extend your right arm to the mat, and reach upward with your left arm. Look up (Figure 7-2). However, if your arm slips off your knee, return to the side prayer.

Figure 7-1 Standing Side Prayer

Extended Side Prayer

Bring both hands to your mat on either side of your feet. Step back with your left leg, into a lunge. The right leg is bent; the left leg straight. Now bring your left foot forward a few inches and turn your heel in at about a thirty-degree angle. Keep the foot flat. Go into the **extended side prayer** position by placing your right elbow inside the right knee and bringing your palms together near your heart as you twist to the left. If this is too challenging, drop your left knee to the mat. If you want to extend further, drop your armpit to your knee (Figure 7-3).

Figure 7-2 Standing Side Stretch

Figure 7-3 Extended Side Prayer

Triangle

Next, go into the **triangle** by straightening your right leg in front of you and dropping your right arm to your ankle or the mat. Reach for the ceiling with your left hand. Look up. Hold for five or six breaths (Figure 7-4).

Figure 7-4 Triangle Position One

Reach your left arm alongside your head just above your left ear. Keep the arm straight so that you form a line between your left heel and your fingertips (Figure 7-5). Take three deep breaths, then reach up again. This time drop your arm back further, opening up your chest. Hold for three more breaths.

Figure 7-5 Triangle Position Two

Figure 7-6 Revolving Triangle

Revolving Triangle

Raise your upper body back to a standing position, keeping your arms extended and your legs apart. Now reverse your arms, bringing the left arm forward and the right arm back. Bend forward and either clasp onto your right ankle or place your hand on the outside of the foot. Stretch your right arm upward as you twist (Figure 7-6).

Reversed Side Prayer

Next, bring both hands to either side of the right foot and drop your left knee to the mat. Take your right hand and move your right knee to the left a few inches. Twist to the right by bringing your left elbow to the outside of your right knee and press your palms together. Keep your right elbow pointing up and your left elbow turned down. Now you're in the **reversed side**

Figure 7-7 Reversed Side Prayer

prayer (Figure 7-7). Hold for five to six breaths. This position may be the most challenging in the series for you.

If you're not familiar with these postures, or they seem very difficult, take your time. Take breaks between the postures, if needed. Do the best you can. With practice, you'll find your body opening up for these side twists.

Repeat the postures on the other side, starting with the mountain and moving into the side prayer on the left side of your body. After you've gone through the postures on both sides of your body, move from form to intent and repeat the postures on each side. Use your keywords—*growth*, *expansion*, *wisdom*, *the big picture*—and pull in the energy related to Sagittarius. If you're doing an abbreviated workout, move into intent after you finish the postures on the first side.

Variations

If the triangle posture is too challenging, you can replace it with the **extended side angle posture**, which allows you to bend the forward leg. Go from the extended side prayer position into the modified side angle stretch by resting your forearm on your thigh and reaching your other arm upward. You can see this posture in

Figure 7-8 Extended Side Angle Posture—Advanced Version

Chapter 17 (Figure 17-4A). From that position, you can also straighten your lower arm and place your palm to the mat inside your foot. Stretch your other arm upward (Figure 17-4B).

You might also incorporate the extended side angle posture into the Sagittarius workout in order to expand on the series. For an advanced version of the posture, reach under your thigh with

Figure 7-9 Reversed Side Prayer with Extended Leg

the lower arm and clasp onto your wrist or hand after you wrap the arm around your back (Figure 7-8).

For a challenging option from the reversed side prayer position, straighten your back knee, coming up on the toes of that foot (Figure 7-9). Next, put your lower hand on the mat and reach up toward the ceiling with your upper arm. Twist (Figure 7-10).

You can also enter the extended reversed side prayer from the standing side prayer by lunging your outside leg back and straightening it. At the same time, lower your hips so that your front thigh is parallel to the floor. You might try this variation

Figure 7-10 Reversed Side Angle Posture

on your last round when you are thoroughly warmed up. But don't attempt it until you have perfected the individual postures, especially the reversed side prayer.

Breath of Fire

After you've finished the postures, you can move to a seated cross-legged position for the Breath of Fire. See Chapter 4 for details.

EARTH

8

Earth: Grounding

We walk on it, cultivate it, grow food in it, plant flowers and grass in it. It holds our dead, our wastes, our garbage. We beautify it, water it, build on it, abuse it, and call it Mother. It remains our stability, timeless and forever, still here long after we are gone. Earth.

Earth is yin, receptive, intuitive. It symbolizes the backbone of fire's creative expression, its practical expression, its grounding. Earth is stable and solid—real in a way that air is not because we can see it, touch it, and sift it through our fingers. Earth is infinitely reliable, here for the long haul. It isn't changeless, however. It shifts and eddies, erupts and crumbles, becomes barren or fertile, warm or cool. These changes, though, usually occur because of the influence of other elements.

Earth sign people are a lot like the earth itself—dependable, practical, thorough, efficient, organized, responsible. Show them a product and they ask: *Does it save time? Energy? Money? Is it useful? How can I make it more efficient and productive? How can I organize this so it makes sense?*

Fire signs discover new worlds, but earth signs cultivate them. George Lucas, a Taurus, cultivated an entire mythology in his *Star Wars* movies and accumulated enormous wealth, another earth trait. Max Perkins, a Virgo, didn't just edit the books of writers like Thomas Wolfe and F. Scott Fitzgerald; he *perfected* the novels, sculpted them into classics. As a result, he became nearly as famous as the authors whose works he tended. Humphrey Bogart, a Capricorn, has been dead for decades, but his legacy has flourished, climbing higher and higher toward the stars.

Where fire signs are the Scarlett O'Haras of the zodiac, earth signs are like Tara itself. Where fire signs leap at risk, earth signs tend to hold back, mulling things over, studying the problem until they fully absorb it. They immerse themselves—then act. They may not have the infectious zeal of fire signs, but when they speak, when they make a decision, when they act, you can rest assured they have thought things through and covered every base. They're the people you want to hire to manage money or human resources.

Many earth signs have a hidden side that is deeply mystical or spiritual. Part of their challenge is to allow this hidden side to surface, and to be more open and up-front about it so they can attract people of like mind. Again, go back to *Star Wars*. The underlying theme that Lucas created is both spiritual and deeply mystical: to harness and master "The Force" for beneficial purposes.

Of the three earth signs, Taurus is most closely linked to the earth. And, since it's ruled by Venus, the goddess of love and romance, it's the most sensual of the earth signs. Virgo is the most intellectual of the three, and Capricorn, the most ambitious. Taurus and Capricorn can be quite physically oriented individuals. Because of their tenacity, they can go up against a sign like Aries in any kind of sport or physical competition and win hands down. Winning, however, doesn't matter to them as much as finishing the competition.

The shadow side of earth signs is their tendency to live as if they're wearing blinders, failing to see how what they do affects the people closest to them. It's not that they lack compassion;

they're simply self-contained, focused on what they're doing and involved in. To signs that move and live quickly—fire and air—earth signs may seem to be too plodding and dilatory. On the other hand, a dash of earthy stability and dependability may be just what fire and air need.

To draw earth energy into your life, you must be very clear about your intent. Exactly what qualities are you seeking? Dependability? Stability? Endurance? Responsibility? The qualities you're hoping to bring into your life are invariably connected to particular situations or issues in your life and it would behoove you to know what they are.

Are these issues related to work? Relationships? Spirituality? Your profession and career? Your family? Your health? Are the issues internal? One Aquarian man, a runner who entered ten-kilometer races on a regular basis, began emphasizing the earth postures in his Astro-Yoga workout. Although he trained for the races, his energy, determination, and stamina invariably faltered during the last few kilometers. His focus wandered, and his body lit up with a litany of complaints. By using his intent and drawing on the energy of the earth postures, Taurus in particular, he was able to increase his endurance so that the last two kilometers were as easy as the first eight. He entered his next race with a new sense of determination. He didn't win or even place among the leaders, but he finished the race feeling strong and beat his own record time by more than thirty seconds.

This man was absolutely clear about his intent, which helped him derive the maximum benefits of Astro-Yoga. Sometimes, though, issues aren't as clear-cut. They spill over into several areas of our lives. It then becomes necessary to distill the essence of the issue or challenge you want to work on.

In the following exercise, jot down the situations or issues in your life that you would like to work on. Even if there's more than one issue, try to keep your statement simple and clear. Then ask yourself what attributes you will need to accomplish this goal. Glance through the lists of traits, checking only the attributes that apply to you and your issues.

Brainstorming

Earth Sign Attributes

The situations or issues that I would like to work on are: ________________

____

Taurus Attributes

Concrete ____________ Reliability ____________

Endurance ____________ Sensuality ____________

Grounded ____________ Serenity ____________

Practicality ____________ Stability ____________

Virgo Attributes

Analytical ____________ Imposing order ____________

Critical ____________ Problem-solving ____________

Detail-oriented ____________ Seeking perfection ____________

Discriminating perceptions ____________ Service to others ____________

Capricorn Attributes

Ambition ____________ Responsibility ____________

Business acumen ____________ Self-discipline ____________

Leadership ____________ Structure ____________

Patience ____________ Traditional values ____________

Areas of my life which pertain to situation or issue

Finances ____________ Spirituality ____________

Personal relationships ____________ Work/profession ____________

General self-improvement ____________

Other notes to myself:

____

____

____

____

____

____

Using the Lists

The lists of attributes stress the most positive aspects of each sign. When you read through the lists, think in terms of your life right now, this instant. If you're honest with yourself, you'll realize that you already have or express some of these traits. Perhaps your family life is flourishing, but your career is lagging. In that case, make sure in the last section of the list you've checked off "work"—or any other area that is appropriate.

The section that has the most check marks indicates the earth sign energy you should work with to address the situations or issues that you jotted at the top of the table. If no area has more checks than any other, select any of the series of postures related to the three earth signs.

Your Body and Earth Signs

In astrology, each sign rules a part of the body, which is considered to be the most vulnerable area for that sign. In personalizing your workout, you may want to periodically include postures that relate to your sign's body part. Taurus, for example, rules the neck and throat, so if you're a Taurus, consider doing postures for your own sign to strengthen the area the sign rules. The following table lists the earth signs and the parts of the body they rule.

Parts of the Body Ruled by Earth Signs

Earth Signs	Part of Body
♉ Taurus, fixed	Throat, neck, ears, cervical vertebrae
♍ Virgo, mutable	Intestines, abdomen, liver, gallbladder
♑ Capricorn, cardinal	Knees, bones, skin, teeth, joints, ligaments

What's Coming Up

In the next three chapters, we'll be discussing the earth signs and describing the Astro-Yoga postures that go with each sign. First, go back to the brainstorming activity in this chapter and review the attributes you've checked. If any sign has more checks than the others, read that sign first, then try the yoga postures.

Ujjayi Breath

The breathing exercise that relates to the earth signs, *Ujjayi*, is practiced either in a seated position with the legs crossed, or in a kneeling position sitting between your feet. Begin by relaxing your neck, shoulders, back, hips, and legs. Feel gravity pulling your body down toward the earth.

Inhale slowly and deeply through your nose with your mouth closed. Partially close the back of your throat, slowing the flow of air. Feel and hear the air moving over the palate at the back of your throat. You should hear a hissing sound, which is somewhat like the sound you hear when you hold a conch shell to your ear. Hold for several seconds, then exhale. Again, feel the breath over your palate and follow the sound of your breath.

The ujjayi breath cleanses the lungs and relaxes the nervous system. It also allows you to increase your endurance if you continue with the breath during the postures.

Before attempting this breath during any posture, practice combining the ujjayi breath with arm and head movements during your breathing exercise. From the same seated position, clasp your hands together beneath your chin bringing your elbows close together. Look straight ahead. Now, as you inhale in the manner described above, slowly raise your elbows out to the sides. When your elbows won't go any further, drop your head back pushing the chin skyward. At this point, you won't be able to inhale any further. Slowly exhale as you bring your elbows together in front of you, then lower your elbows and chin until you are looking straight ahead again.

9

Taurus, the Bull

Theme:
To maintain serenity
Keywords:
Persistence, determination, stability, security
April 20–May 20
Ruled by Venus
Fixed earth
Rules throat, neck, cervical vertebrae

Perseverance is what the energy of Taurus is all about. Forget speed born of impatience. Forget deadlines. Taurus energy moves at its own pace. But long after other signs have given up, Taurus remains in the race, leaving no stone unturned. Nothing is overlooked. One way or another, this energy finishes what it starts.

Taurus energy is what you need when you're facing daunting tasks or difficult decisions. In a situation where you must stand firm in your own beliefs, this energy is invaluable.

Serenity is intrinsic to the Taurus individual. She needs external peace to find inner peace. As a result, many bulls are lovers of the outdoors, whose primary lessons in life come from Mother Nature. Hikes, rock climbing, windsurfing, camping, traveling in the wild: welcome to the bull's world.

Within this world, there isn't a whole lot of chatter. She doesn't like being around people who talk just to hear the sound of their own voice. Endless chatter disrupts the serenity she seeks. As a result, she rarely discusses what she feels; it's enough to simply feel it, to allow that feeling to permeate her senses. It's nothing personal, you understand. In fact, if you have a genuine problem, she's a good listener. But don't expect her to come to you with *her* problems. When she's feeling blue, she's apt to head into the woods, or to the beach to watch the sun rise, or she finds a physical outlet, such as yoga.

Taurus, in fact, is one of the most physical signs, with a highly tuned sense of touch. She needs to touch things to define and understand them. Gardening, cooking, playing an instrument, sculpting, lovemaking, hugging a tree or a child. Her body is a vehicle of transformation, a cause for celebration.

Some astrologers believe that Taurus is actually ruled by the Earth, not by Venus, and there seems to be some truth to this. She is the earthiest of signs, the prototypical earth mother, her embrace large enough to encompass the world beyond her own—as long as it doesn't violate her serenity. The influence of Venus, however, is also evident in the bull. Her sensuality is the means through which she acquaints herself with the world. Sex may be a form of communication for other signs, but for Taurus, it is first and foremost about touch and feeling good.

Take food, for example. To a Taurus, food isn't something you eat just to keep you going; to Taurus, it's a delight, an experience to be savored. Many Taureans, in fact, are terrific cooks, whipping up gourmet masterpieces with dazzling effortlessness—a dash of exotic herbs, a splash of wine, a pinch of something you can't pronounce and, voilà, the six-course meal is laid out in front of you.

The Taurean sensuality is apparent in most areas of her life. Her home or office isn't just a place to live or work—it's a personal environment that intimately reflects who she really is. Walk into her house or her office and it's likely that you'll hear music playing softly in the background. You probably won't find boldly colored walls in her home or office—no purples or reds;

these are too outlandish for her stylish tastes. But you will find pastels and, here and there, splashes of color. In fact, Feng Shui probably holds an intuitive appeal for her.

Taurus is a romantic—this holds true for both men and women. They enjoy the seduction of romance, the flow of it. But once they commit, it's generally a "come hell or high water" type of commitment. However, if Taurus feels you don't really appreciate her, if you're not willing to take the time to make her feel loved, then she'll be gone like the wind and don't expect to see her again. Remember: Taurus is a fixed sign, the most stubborn in the zodiac. Once she makes a decision, very little can change her mind.

She's fairly even-tempered most of the time, but if you push her too far, be prepared for the legendary bull's rush, an explosion of fury that is sure to send you in the opposite direction very quickly. In fact, even if you're in the mood to scream it out, don't. Back off to prevent yourself from saying something that will wound Taurus so deeply she may never forget it. Even though she isn't known for holding grudges, her memory for emotional injury is remarkably lucid. Despite appearances to the contrary, she is incredibly sensitive.

Part of the secret of Taurus's legendary staying power is that she knows how to pace herself. This allows her to avoid the burnout that hits other signs. Her metabolism also seems to be slower than signs like Aries and Gemini, so she's rarely in a big hurry to get somewhere or do something. And yet, when a Taurus is on deadline, she pulls out all the stops and does whatever is necessary to make it on time.

Think of the grandest tree you've ever seen—an oak, perhaps, or a California redwood. That's Taurus, fixed and solid, rooted in the same spot forever. And that's the catch for this sign, the shadow side. Taurus's serenity can be all mixed up with security issues. If she sticks to the job she detests, she will be able to retire at fifty-five with a pension plan, money in the bank, and great health and life insurance. But her heart yearns for her own business, a music store with a café, a place where music lovers can browse and talk from morning to midnight. If she follows the yearning of her heart, her security goes straight out the window. But if she stays with her job, she may die from boredom.

This conflict is the essential pivot of Taurus's life, the inevitable crossroad that she reaches. Ifs, ands, and buts become her litany. To stay, remain secure, and possibly stagnate, or to take the leap of faith: which will it be?

Building a Personalized Workout

Back to polarities. Taurus/Scorpio. The bull is yin, the scorpion is yang. Taurus is Kevin Spacey in *American Beauty*; Scorpio is Kathleen Turner in *Body Heat*. Taurus seeks serenity, Scorpio seeks transformation at the deepest levels. While they can't coexist, they need each other, and they are attracted to each other because each fills the other's void.

We probably will never convince a Taurus that she needs any energy except her own—unless she comes to that conclusion herself. That said, if you are a Taurus, read the Scorpio chapter and the brainstorming list for water signs. You may find that you want to include Scorpio postures in your workout.

If your checklist suggests that you need some serenity and stability in your life, then read through these postures before you try them. When you do them for the first time, listen to your body. What is it telling you about the postures? Do you have any emotional reaction to them? The second time you do the postures, do them with intent.

Intent affirmation: *I now pull serenity and stability into my life. I am grounded.*

Tailor the words to fit your needs. Maybe you need sensuality in your life. Maybe you need to develop reliability. Whatever the qualities you're seeking, create the affirmation that feels right for you, right now.

Intent visualization: The temptation here may be to use a bull as the symbol of what you want. While an animal symbol works for some signs, don't limit yourself. The visualization part of the process should be imaginative, vivid, created in the spirit of where you are at this moment in your life. The visualization and affirmation should change as your needs change.

Lydia, a woman in her early fifties, is a Sagittarian with four grown kids. At the time that she started doing yoga, her life was in flux, in transition. She and her husband were in the midst of a divorce, her kids were having problems, and she'd just been fired from her job. She was so desperately in need of stability that yoga quickly became a stable point in her chaotic life. When we personalized her workout, the Taurus postures were at the top of our list.

To maintain the Taurean energy on a daily basis, we recommended that she design an affirmation and visualization that fit her overt need for stability. If and when she found herself in stressful situations where yoga postures were inappropriate, she could say the affirmation or do her visualization to ground herself, to stabilize herself.

In her affirmation, she used some of the keywords for Taurus. She said that she was stable, secure, and well-grounded. In her visualization, she created an image of herself as a large tree with deep roots. While the image might seem odd, it helped to give her a sense of stability that she drew on during her Taurean workout and throughout the day. Although she also practiced other series for the physical benefits, she only used her intent during the cobra/downward-facing dog series, when she could use her affirmation and visualization.

Both the affirmation and visualization become second nature if you practice them often enough and with genuine sincerity. They will see you through just about any stressful situation.

The Cobra/Downward-Facing Dog Series

Taurus epitomizes stamina and endurance, and this series builds both qualities. The downward-facing dog, at the heart of the series, enhances upper body strength while bringing more blood to the brain. The posture strengthens the abdominals and legs and energizes the body. The palms and the soles of the feet are grounded and connected with the earth. The counter posture, the cobra, or upward-facing dog, tones the entire spine, corrects poor posture, and stretches the muscles from the lower back to the neck and shoulders. This posture also increases circulation to the spine and aids in digestion.

Dog/Cat Tilt

Begin in the table position on your hands and knees with your shoulders over your hands. Raise your head and arch your back as you inhale through the nose. Hold the **dog tilt** (Figure 9-1) for two or three breaths. Then exhale, round your back, and drop your head, stretching into the **cat tilt** (Figure 9-2). Go back and forth between the postures at least three times as you stretch and contract the abdominal muscles and flex the spine.

The Sphinx

Slide back from the table position into the extended-arm child's pose (see Figure 6-6). Now slide forward, keeping your chin just above the mat and your back arched until your head comes between your hands. Next, slide your knees back, straightening your legs and coming onto your belly. Relax a few moments with your forehead on the mat. Then, press down with your hands and forearms and raise your head and chest as you come into the **sphinx** (Figure 9-3). Hold for five or six breaths, then lower down.

Now try the floating sphinx. Raise your forearms an inch or two off the mat, then lift your head and chest. Hold for three or four breaths.

The Cobra

Slide your hands next to your chest. Press down and raise your head and chest into the **cobra**. Remember to keep your elbows in, your shoulders back, and your hips and thighs on the mat (Figure 9-4). Hold for five or six breaths. For a more challenging variation, place your hands along your sides just below the rib cage.

Figure 9-1
Dog Tilt

Figure 9-2
Cat Tilt

Downward-Facing Dog

Bring your shoulders over your hands as you lift your hips and come into the plane position. Keep your legs, back, and neck in a straight line. After a momentary pause, push back through your tailbone, forming an inverted V as you press your palms down and your heels toward the floor in the **downward-facing dog** (Figure 9-5).

Figure 9-3
The Sphinx

Figure 9-4
The Cobra

If you're not accustomed to this position, first keep your knees slightly bent and work to push the crown of your head toward the mat. Your shoulder blades should squeeze together as you arch your back. Stretch your calves by bending one knee, then the other, pushing the opposite heel down. Raise up on your toes and hold several seconds, then push both heels down. If you can't get them all the way to the floor, walk your feet in a little closer and try again. With practice, the crown of your head moves toward the floor and you look toward your feet.

Hold the downward-facing dog for at least five or six breaths, then either move into the next posture or take a break by dropping to your knees.

Figure 9-5 Downward-Facing Dog

Figure 9-6 Upward-Facing Dog

Upward-Facing Dog

Go into the plane position again, then move your hips down and forward. This posture differs from the cobra in that you keep your hips and thighs off the mat. Bring your shoulders back and your chest forward as you arch your back. You can either let your knees touch the mat or you can keep your knees raised (Figure 9-6). You'll quickly realize that the **upward-facing dog** requires more upper body strength than the cobra. If this posture is too challenging, substitute it with the cobra. Hold for five or six breaths.

Repeat the downward-facing dog and upward-facing dog combination again, then drop to your hands and knees in the table position and slide back toward your heels in the extended-arm child's pose. Slide forward onto your belly again.

Upward Boat

Extend your arms in front of you and point your toes. When you're ready, inhale and raise your arms, head, and chest as well as your legs. Hold the **upward boat** for three or four breaths (Figure 9-7). Repeat the posture, but this time, after three or four breaths, extend your arms out to the sides (Figure 9-8).

Figure 9-7 Upward Boat

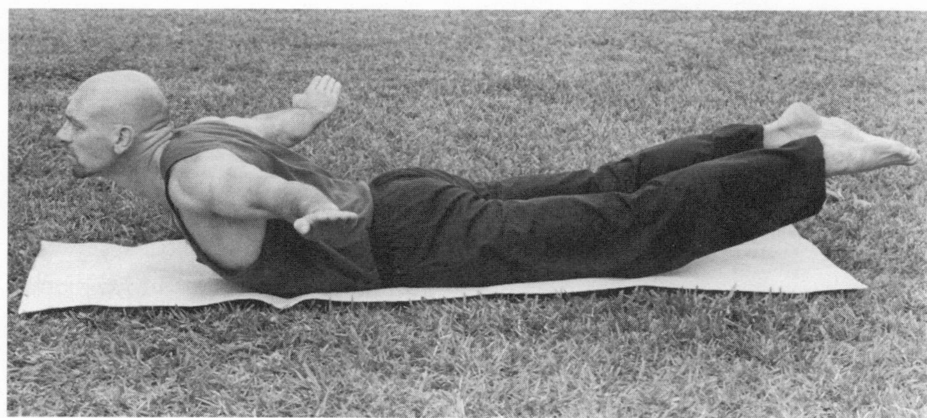

Figure 9-8 Upward Boat Variation

The Bow Posture

Figure 9-9 The Bow

Release the upward boat posture by relaxing your arms. When you're ready to move on to the next posture in the series, bend your knees and reach back for your ankles. Arch your back and raise your chest and legs as high as they can go. The **bow** posture tones the abdominal organs, including the liver, spleen, and kidneys, and also makes the spine more supple. Hold for five or six breaths (Figure 9-9).

Headstand

You can complete the Taurus series with the **headstand**. It's another inverted posture, like the downward-facing dog, and reverses the normal effects of gravity by bringing more oxygen-rich blood to the brain. The posture builds upper body strength, improves concentration and balance, and energizes and activates the entire body.

If you're not used to doing the posture, you might get someone to spot you. But avoid relying on a wall for support, because the arched position could cause excessive strain to the neck.

From your hands and knees, drop the crown of your head down to the mat and clasp your hands together behind your head. Press your forearms to the mat and make sure that they are no wider apart than the width of your shoulders. Now straighten your legs and walk your feet in closer so that your tailbone is almost directly above your head (Figure 9-10A).

Bend your knees and raise your lower body up so that your spine is vertical (Figure 9-10B). Then raise the legs straight overhead (Figure 9-10C). If you're not used to the posture, hold for three or four breaths and come down. Work to hold the posture longer and longer.

Figure 9-10A Headstand Position One

Figure 9-10B Headstand Position Two

Figure 9-10C Headstand Position Three

If the inverted posture is too challenging, you can gain upper body strength by practicing the downward-facing dog on your forearms. (Read the description of this posture, known as the dolphin, in Chapter 18 and see Figure 18-7.)

After you come down from the headstand, relax and prepare yourself for the intent phase. Focus on your personal affirmation and visualization or the keywords for Taurus: *persistence*, *determination*, *stability*, *commitment*. Think about how you can apply the energy of Taurus in your daily life. Then move into your postures again, saying the keywords as you go.

Variation

Once you're in the downward-facing dog, lift one leg up and push the opposite heel to the mat. Switch legs and repeat with each leg three or four times. Begin by raising the leg parallel to the floor, then as you progress, try raising it higher and higher. For another challenging posture from the downward-facing dog position, bring one knee to your chest, then slide forward so that your shoulders are above your hands and hold for three or four breaths. Push back and repeat with the other leg.

In place of the bow, or in addition to it, you can include the locust posture. Facing downward on your belly, slide your arms beneath you with the palms down. Bring your elbows in as close as possible, and push your chin out. Start with the half-locust by raising one leg as high as you can. Hold for three or four breaths. Switch legs. Next, practice the full locust by lifting both legs as you press down with your palms. Keep your elbows in as best you can. Hold for two or three breaths. With practice, hold the posture for a longer time.

Ujjayi Breath

After you've completed the series, you can relax on your back for the breathing exercise related to the earth signs (see Chapter 8).

10

Virgo, the Virgin

Theme:
Seeking perfection
Keywords:
Service, details, perfection
August 23–September 22
Ruled by Mercury
Mutable earth
Rules intestines and abdomen

Details: this is Virgo's domain. No sign is more proficient at connecting the dots, but this attention to details is part of a larger quest for perfection of self, a kind of inner search for the best that one can be. Virgo is also connected with health and hygiene, daily work conditions, and work in general—as opposed to a profession.

In his quest for perfection, the Virgo individual sculpts and molds his experiences, arranging and rearranging the pieces, until the end result actually benefits everyone involved. That's the beauty of it. What begins as a personal quest becomes something much larger than himself and ultimately transforms the lives of everyone around him.

There are, for instance, an inordinate number of Virgo individuals in publishing—Virgo suns, moons, ascendants, and a predominance of Virgo planets. From an astrological point of view, this makes perfect sense. Analytical and critical thought—the left brain—organizes what is essentially right-brain material. What the right brain creates, the left brain streamlines. This process *serves others*—the writer, the publisher, and the reader. In many instances, this process also changes mass thinking, impacting us as a society, a nation, and a world.

But let's bring it down to everyday life. You're driving through the worst section of town, late at night, and your battery dies. You've got enough power left in your cell phone to make one call. Who do you call? Not ghostbusters. Not AAA, the cops, or even your mother. Your call goes to your Virgo buddy, who answers the phone with a frog in his throat that makes it abundantly clear he's been asleep for hours. But Virgo responds like a trooper: twenty minutes later, he's at the site of your personal disaster, jump-starting your battery. If it's summer, he has brought cold water; if it's winter, he's got a blanket to keep you warm.

To Virgo, every problem has a solution, and rescues in the middle of the night are simply things that you do for friends. He doesn't expect compensation; he is pleased to be of service.

Virgo has been unnecessarily maligned by astrologers in the past. Fussy about details (makes a terrific accountant) or, even worse, prissy and overly critical. These descriptions make Virgo sound incapable of change and growth, but nothing is further from the truth.

As a mutable earth sign, he is driven by a vision of what might be, an ideal that compels him to perfect whatever he takes on. It's all a work in progress to Virgo. He, like Michaelangelo, seeks to release the ideal from the potential, the image from the stone. In doing this, he masters details, the minutiae, because he knows that perfection doesn't lie only in what you see; to be truly perfect, to become the ideal, requires perfection even in the intricacies that aren't apparent to the naked eye.

Virgo is unusually efficient in whatever he takes on. His eye for detail invariably allows him to fix things so that they work better—a job, an appliance, a relationship, even himself. Make it practical. Make it better than it is. Self-criticism is, in fact, part of Virgo's shadow side. His quest for the ideal is never as rigorous as when he applies it to himself. *I'm not good enough, not smart enough, not educated enough.* He is brutal on himself, and if the cycle continues, it eventually extends to other people.

This cycle ultimately leads to self-sacrifice, which is manifested in any number of ways: the workaholic who feels he must work twenty-two hours a day to make the grade or the spouse who suffers abuse in silence . . . you get the idea here. In the cycle of self-sacrifice, Virgo becomes trapped in detail. He can't see the forest because he's stuck in the trees. He becomes his own worst enemy.

Virgo's challenge is to love himself, as he exists now, in this moment. One of the ways he learns to do this is through his work. It's the means through which he can unravel the labyrinth of his own mind. After all, Mercury rules this sign and Mercury is about the mind, the intellect, communication in all of its forms. Mercury is the messenger.

Mercury also rules Gemini, Virgo's mutable cousin, and although the two are intellectually compatible, their differences are pronounced. Gemini is driven by curiosity; Virgo is driven by the need to fit the pieces together so they form the ideal. Once he learns to love himself as he is now, in this instant, attainment of the ideal is just a heartbeat away.

Building a Personalized Workout

Virgo's polar opposite is Pisces. They have mental flexibility in common, but not much else. Like any pair of opposites, each supplies what the other lacks, which creates a delicate energy fulcrum. Virgo is left brained, Pisces is right brained. Virgo sees the trees and Pisces sees not just the forest, but the forest as a living, breathing entity. Virgo's analytical mind needs that kind of mystical softening.

If you're reading this chapter because you're a Virgo, then turn to the Pisces chapter and read through those postures and include them in your regular workout. If you're reading this chapter because the brainstorming activity suggests that you need some of Virgo's energy, read through the postures first, then try them on for size. How does your body feel when you do the postures? How do you feel emotionally? Note the ease or difficulty of the postures. Develop awareness about what your body is saying, then repeat the postures with *intent.*

Intent affirmation: *I now bring order and critical thinking into my life.*

Again, tailor your affirmation to fit what you're hoping to pull into your life. Play around with the words until they feel right.

Intent visualization: What constitutes *ideal* for you in the area you're working on? You have to define this ideal before you can visualize it. Forget left-brain definitions; this process requires that you draw on Piscean energy for guidance. Ask for a dream that defines, or, at the very least, illuminates the ideal. If you meditate, pose the question during meditation. However you approach it, the answer should be something that comes from you—not your family and friends, not your professional associates, not your therapist. This is your visualization, your process. Claim your power, then put it to work for you.

The Forward Bend Series

In this series, you're stretching toward the earth, and reaching for the energy of Virgo. But what if your back is stiff and your hamstrings are so short that you don't even come close to reaching your mat? Does that make you less able to draw in the energy of Virgo? Not at all. While increased flexibility is certainly desirable, the stiff and inflexible can draw in the energy of Virgo, or any other sign, just as easily as those who are as flexible as noodles.

Since the forward bend series is practiced from a seated position, it tends to be somewhat passive. That means the positions are held longer, there are fewer of them, and they are not as fluid and flowing as the more active series. As a result, the Virgo series is more meditative, allowing you longer periods to focus your intent on the earth energy of the sign.

Pick out three or four of the postures to begin with and either work up to five or six of them, or vary them from session to session. The forward bend postures tone the spinal column, strengthen the abdominal organs, and lengthen the shoulder muscles. The series also invigorates the entire nervous system, helps process waste in the kidneys, and improves digestion.

When you've completed the form segment, use your intent and the keywords to pull in Virgo's energy: *seeking perfection, attending to details, problem-solving, service to others.* Don't just say the words, but personalize them to fit your own circumstances. Where do you need this energy in your life? Use your visualization to focus on the end result you desire.

Forward Bend

Begin in a seated position with your legs straight out in front of you. Sit up straight and press your hands into the floor next to your hips. Keep your shoulders back.

Inhale and reach up overhead. As you exhale, stretch forward, lengthening your spine, but only go about halfway down. Reach another inch or two. Take three breaths, then inhale and reach up. Now exhale, bend, and stretch. Clasp whatever you can reach, your knees, calves, ankles, or feet. Inhale and look up, pushing your belly toward your thighs; this massages your internal organs. Exhale and round down, folding toward your legs (Figure 10-1). Take five or six breaths as you hold the **forward bend** posture.

Figure 10-1 Forward Bend

Foot-to-Thigh Bend

Again, from a seated position, bend your left knee and place your foot on the inside of your thigh, letting the knee drop toward the mat. Inhale, raise your arms, then bend forward at the waist and exhale as you reach with your hands toward your extended foot. Grab whatever you can reach, whether it's your knee, calf, ankle, or foot (Figure 10-2). If your knee remains off the mat, you can release your left hand from your leg or foot and press down on your left knee, stretching your hip as you lengthen your spine into the **foot-to-thigh bend**. Hold the posture for five or six breaths, then switch legs.

Alternately, if your hips are flexible enough so that your knee touches the mat, then you can place your right ankle on top of your left thigh in the half-lotus, then fold down toward your leg (Figure 10-3).

Figure 10-2 Foot-to-Thigh Bend

Figure 10-3 *Half*-Lotus Forward Bend

Foot-to-Hip Bend

Start the same way as the previous posture, but this time place your right heel near your right hip. You can either place the side of your foot or the top of your foot on the mat. Inhale, raising your arms overhead, then exhale and bend forward. The **foot-to-hip bend** stretches your foot and ankle as well as your hip (Figure 10-4). However, anyone with knee problems should proceed cautiously when entering this posture. Hold for five or six breaths, and switch legs.

Figure 10-4 Foot-to-Hip Bend

Figure 10-5 Knee-Raised Bend

Knee-Raised Bend

Begin the **knee-raised bend** from a seated position with both legs extended. Bend your left knee, placing your foot firmly down beneath it. Now wrap your left arm around the outside of your calf and thigh and your right arm around your back. Clasp your hands together against your lower back. Press your left foot down and lean forward (Figure 10-5). Hold for five or six breaths, then change legs and repeat.

Spread-Legged Forward Bend

Next, bring your legs apart as far as you can. Inhale, reach up, turn your torso toward your right leg, then fold down into the **spread-legged forward bend**. Clasp your calf, ankle, or foot. Hold for five or six breaths. Inhale, reach up, then bend down to your left leg and hold again for another five or six breaths.

Figure 10-6 Spread-Legged Forward Bend

Figure 10-7 Spread-Legged Forward Bend Variation

Inhale and reach up. Then exhale and bend forward between your spread legs, reaching out as far as you can to the mat (Figure 10-6). Hold for five or six breaths. Alternately, to gain more leverage, you can clasp your hands onto your ankles or feet and fold forward (Figure 10-7).

Side Bend

Keep your legs spread apart and bend your left knee, bringing the foot in toward the groin. Reach up with your left arm and come down sideways toward your right leg. Extend your right hand toward your foot (Figure 10-8). For a deeper stretch, slide your right forearm inside your calf to the mat, drop your left shoulder back, and reach for your foot with your left hand. Hold the **side bend** for five or six breaths.

Extended-Leg Back Arch

As a counter pose, move into the **extended leg back arch**: extend your left arm above your head, then swing your arm back and plant your hand on the mat behind your left hip. Press down with your left hand and lift your buttocks up from the mat; raise your right arm up and back. You are opening your chest and stretching your shoulder, hip, and thigh (Figure 10-9). Hold for three or four breaths.

Switch legs. Repeat the side bend on the left side and follow up again with the extended-leg back arch.

Figure 10-8 Side Bend

Figure 10-9 Extended-Leg Back Arch

Variations

One of the more challenging forward bends is the **foot-to-head** pose. You might need considerable practice before accomplishing this posture, but almost everyone can take the first step, called **rock-the-baby**.

From a seated position, pick up your right ankle with your right hand and place the bottom of your foot inside your left elbow. Release your ankle and wrap your right arm around your knee. Clasp your hands together. Now pull your leg in toward your chest and rock the leg from side to side (Figure 10-10). If you can't get your arms around your leg as described, hold the leg up as best you can and rock.

Next, place your right palm underneath your heel and hold your toes with your left hand. Raise your heel toward your chin. If you can, bring your heel to your nose, then your forehead, then

Figure 10-10 Rock-the-Baby

Figure 10-11A Foot-to-Head Pose Position One

Figure 10-11B Foot-to-Head Pose Position Two

the crown of the head (Figure 10-11A). Next, slide your ankle over the back of your neck (Figure 10-11B). Finally, if you've reached this point, bend at the waist and sink down toward your extended leg. You've done it!

Ujjayi Breath

After you've completed the series, you can relax on your back for the breathing exercise related to the earth signs. See Chapter 8.

11

Capricorn, the Goat

Theme:
Attainment
Keywords:
Ambition, structure, self-discipline
December 22–January 19
Ruled by Saturn
Cardinal earth
Rules knees, skin, bones

Capricorn energy is tireless, indefatigable, and infinitely patient. These qualities are embodied in the symbol for the sign—the goat. True, the symbol isn't quite as pleasing as, say, the Aquarian water-bearer. But it aptly describes the nature of Capricorn as she makes her slow, steady climb to whatever she imagines as the pinnacle.

This energy is what you should tap if your career isn't going where you want it to go, if you're changing professions, or if you're facing some sort of long-range project at work or in your personal life (see Appendix A for other situations that might call for Capricorn energy).

Like her earth sibling, Virgo, Capricorn is an industrious worker, but for different reasons. Where Virgo works to perfect himself and to reach his ideal, Capricorn works to attain her goals. Her serious manner is usually evident even when she's quite young, as if she were a 40-year-old in a 10-year-old's body.

Life itself is serious business for Capricorn. It's a strategy, a plan, a journey which must take her from point A to point Z in a focused way. Deviations from the route she lays out aren't permitted, as there's not much time to play. This type of approach is begun in early childhood, so if you're the parent of a Capricorn child, the greatest gift you can give her is the ability to laugh and have fun.

Capricorns enjoy solitary sports nearly as much as Tauruses do, but not necessarily because nature refreshes them. Their solitude is the point. They enjoy their own company, perhaps because it allows them to put some distance between themselves and that looming mountaintop they haven't quite reached yet.

An element of materialism is evident in many Capricorns. This isn't negative unless the emphasis is on money and things strictly for status and prestige. If she's driving a Lexus or BMW because she thinks it elevates her in other people's eyes, then she's better off driving a VW. If she's married to a millionaire and lives in a grand house, but is utterly miserable and lonely, then she's better off divorced and alone. In other words, to avoid entering the shadow side of her nature, Capricorn should be acutely aware of her own motives. If she's not, then materialism collapses into outright greed, ambition becomes all-consuming, and she loses sight of the summit she hopes to reach.

Capricorns tend to be worriers. We all know the type—the insomniac who wears a midnight path between the bedroom and the kitchen, or the parent who frets about the worst possible scenario when a son or daughter is fifteen minutes late. Blame Saturn, the planet that rules the sign. Saturn is the taskmaster, the planet weighted with responsibility, rules, regulations, and structure. Nothing drives a Capricorn crazy faster than someone who breaks the rules and refuses to function within the structure she has created.

In business, whether home-based or otherwise, Capricorn is an excellent strategist and delegator. She lays out a plan, maps the route, and delegates responsibilities to people she trusts. She never expects more of her employees than she herself is willing to give. Problems arise, however, when her employees balk at working twenty-hour days. Those who can't tow the line soon learn just how cold and detached she can be.

It's rare that a Capricorn will blow up; the Aries fire simply isn't in her. She's more likely to just freeze you out or glare at you with eyes of granite. Even if the misunderstanding blows over, she isn't likely to forget what set her off—and she won't let you forget it, either. The good news is that she probably won't hold it against you.

Capricorns tend to be thrifty, building their fortunes the same way they build their careers, with scrupulous planning, one penny at a time. If they invest in stocks, they do so conservatively. They usually know to the penny what's in their retirement portfolios. Notable exceptions to this rule occur when the natal moon is in a flamboyant sign like Leo or a restless sign like Aries or Gemini.

Capricorn has trouble trusting "the process," whatever it might be. She must learn that she can't control every facet of her life or of the lives of the people she loves. If she can loosen up a bit and take a leap of faith, the rewards she reaps will be enormous.

Building a Personalized Workout

A goat and a crab—how can any two creatures be more different? Yet, Capricorn and Cancer, its polar opposite, share a strange attraction. Both are cardinal signs, so they use energy in the same way, and on a purely physical level, their movements are actually similar.

A goat doesn't scale a mountain by going straight up; it goes first in one direction and then in the opposite direction. A crab rarely moves in a straight line, either. It darts to the left and the right, making its way across a beach in diagonals.

On a more esoteric level, their movements are also similar. Where Capricorn climbs summits, seeking attainment in the outer world, Cancer travels inward with the same determination, seeking to unravel her myriad emotions and intuitive impressions. Both seek security, but in different forms.

If you're a Capricorn, read the Cancer chapter and glance through the water brainstorming activities. Consider including the Cancer postures—the moon salutation—in your personalized workout.

If you're reading the Capricorn chapter because the brainstorming activities indicate you need this type of energy, then read through the postures before you try them. The first time you do the postures, be aware of how you feel physically, emotionally, intellectually, spiritually. Take inventory. When you go through the postures the second time, do them with *intent.*

Intent affirmation: *I now pull ambition and self-discipline into my life.*

Create an affirmation that suits your needs. In the brainstorming section, maybe you checked business acumen and leadership; if so, use those words. The point is to create an affirmation that is simple, easy to remember, and addresses your needs for *right now.*

Intent visualization: The visualization you create depends entirely on what type of characteristics you're trying to draw into your life. Do you need more structure? Do you want more traditional values? More patience? Regardless of the traits you need, the visualization should be something vivid and simple. Something that is all yours.

Once you become accustomed to the affirmation and visualization, you can use them anywhere—before going to a job interview, before making a presentation, before hiring or firing someone. In those types of situations, you may not have the opportunity to do the postures, so at least say the affirmation and allow the visualization to permeate your senses.

A kind of alchemy occurs when you use your body as a vehicle for transforming your life. You may not feel it immediately, but you will feel it at some point and suddenly look around at your life and marvel at the changes that have taken place.

The Pigeon/Spinal Twist Series

We're not sure what a pigeon has to do with a goat, but like the Virgo and Taurus series, this series is clearly related to the earth. While a pigeon is a winged creature, we often see this bird on the ground. In fact, pigeons seem more at home walking the earth than flying above it.

Most of the postures are in a prone or seated position, so much of the body is in contact with the earth. The pigeon posture strengthens and stretches the spine, hips, thighs, and groin. It also opens the chest and massages the kidneys and adrenal glands. The spinal twist postures add strength and suppleness to the spine. They also massage the internal organs and stretch the neck and shoulder muscles.

Child's Pose

We begin this series in the **child's pose** sitting on your heels with your forehead on the mat. Your arms can be at your sides or extended in front of you (Figure 11-1).

Figure 11-1 Child's Pose—Extended Arm

Figure 11-2 Upright Pigeon

Upright Pigeon

Next, come up onto your hands and knees in the table position. Slide your left knee forward and your right leg back as your hips sink down toward the mat. To enhance the **upright pigeon** stretch, clasp your left foot with your right hand and pull it to the right. The higher you slide your left foot, the more you will feel the stretch (Figure 11-2). Hold for five or six breaths.

Extended Pigeon

Now extend your arms forward and sink your chest down toward your calf. Stretch an inch or two longer, and feel your arms, chest, and thighs pressing down into the mat. Then relax, and take another five or six breaths (Figure 11-3).

Bent-Knee Forward Bend

Raise up into the upright pigeon again, hold for two breaths, swing your right leg in a half-circle so that your left foot comes into your right thigh. Inhale and reach up, then exhale and fold down, extending your chest to your thigh and your hands toward your foot (Figure 11-4). Hold the **bent-knee forward bend** for five or six breaths.

Figure 11-3 Extended Pigeon

Figure 11-4 Bent-Knee Forward Bend

Spinal Twist

For the **spinal twist**, straighten your left leg, bend your right knee, and bring your foot over your left thigh, planting your foot on the mat. Now place your left hand on your raised knee, extend your right arm in front of you. Next, make a half-circle to the right with your right arm. Then, place your right hand behind your right hip and bring your left elbow over the outside of the raised right knee. Twist and look over your right shoulder. If you want to try a more advanced version, bend your left knee and bring your foot to your right hip (Figure 11-5A).

Avoid hunching over. If you can keep an arch in your spine and you want to enhance the stretch, straighten your left arm and reach for your left knee (Figure 11-5B). For an even more challenging

Figure 11-5A Spinal Twist Position One

Figure 11-5B Spinal Twist Position Two

Figure 11-5C Spinal Twist Position Three

posture, slide your left arm under your raised thigh and wrap your right hand behind your back. Clasp your fingers together or reach for your wrists (Figure 11-5C). Note that in the photo, the legs and arms are in the reversed position. Whichever option you choose, hold the position for five or six breaths.

Hero Position

Finish the series with the **hero position**. Bring your right knee over your left. Square your hips to the floor and reach for your feet (Figure 11-6). Hold again for five or six breaths. For a more challenging position, bow forward toward your legs, but keep your buttocks planted firmly down.

After the hero, come back into the child's pose. Relax down and prepare to use your intent. Focus on the theme of Capricorn: *Attainment*. What goal do you want to attain? As you move into the postures again, say the keywords to yourself: *structure*, *self-discipline*, *ambition*. Now, as you continue, you will work the

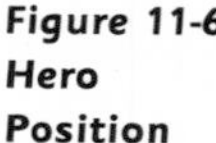

Figure 11-6 Hero Position

opposite side of the body. Follow the instructions of the postures above, but reverse the legs.

Variations

For a somewhat more challenging start to the series, you can enter the pigeon from the downward-facing dog posture (see Figure 9-5). Lunge your foot toward your opposite hand. For example, your right foot lunges to the left hand, and your knee drops toward the other hand. Slide your other knee back as you come into the pigeon.

For more variations of the pigeon, start from the extended pigeon position with your right leg forward. Then twist your upper body to the right and bring your palms together in front of your chest (Figure 11-7). Take three or four breaths, then plant your right hand down and extend your left arm to the right and drop down toward your left shoulder (Figure 11-8). Hold for three or four breaths.

From the upright pigeon, with your right leg forward, extend your left arm in front of you. Now reach back with your right hand and grip your left ankle. Stretch. Hold the **balancing pigeon** for three or four breaths (Figure 11-9).

Figure 11-7 Pigeon Variation

Figure 11-8 Pigeon Variation

Figure 11-9 Balancing Pigeon

Ujjayi Breath

After completing the intent round of the series, you can rest on your back for the breathing exercise related to the earth signs. See Chapter 8.

Air

12

AIR: THE MIND

It's invisible. Yet, we feel it against our skins as hot or cold, cool or warm, pleasant or unpleasant. We see its effects when it rustles through a palm tree, rattling the fronds like castanets, or when a dust devil whirls up the street. It makes our planet habitable. Without it, we wouldn't live more than a few minutes.

Air.

In astrology, air symbolizes the mind, ideas, thought processes, communication, perception, awareness, and learning. Gemini, Libra, Aquarius. They are a collective, a family linked not by blood or DNA, but by intellect.

Although air is essential to our survival, it's also as ephemeral as an angel. When our daughter was two, we snapped a photograph of her smelling a pink hibiscus flower. What stands out in memory isn't the flower or the fact that she was smelling it: it's the way the wind was blowing through her fine blond hair. An effect. A perception. That's the essential quality of air.

Air signs are also concerned with information. Geminis, for instance, have an ease in acquiring and disseminating information. They seem to know something about virtually everything, even though that knowledge is sometimes superficial. Their curiosity propels them. Librans weigh, balance, and compare information, then apply what they learn to relationships. Aquarians apply information and knowledge to universal principles.

Air sign people are often as ephemeral as the element itself. Just when you think you know them, they do or say something that astonishes you, that forces you to realize you don't know them at all, that you may not have even scratched the surface of who they really are. Part of the reason lies in their intrinsic unpredictability. Never mistake an air sign's cheerfulness, charm, and amiability as an indicator that they're pushovers.

The shadow side of air signs is that they are too ambivalent (Gemini), too willing to play both ends against the middle (Libra), or too intellectual and emotionally detached (Aquarius). Of the three, Geminis are most frequently accused of being scatterbrained and superficial. Libra is most often mentioned as the sign that seeks peace at any cost, and Aquarians are viewed as so cold they put the needs of strangers before the needs of their loved ones. But these shadow sides of air signs are mitigated with the development of perception and insight into personal motives.

Fire signs leap at risk, earth signs hold back, and air signs intellectualize it, weaving intricate reasons for pursuing, or not pursuing, a particular course. They're generally able to see the many sides of an issue. This can be an advantage to an individual who acts first and asks questions later, or to someone who has gone through life in a single-minded fashion.

The traits of all signs are defined to some degree by the planet that rules them. Mercury, the messenger, rules Gemini; Venus, goddess of love, rules Libra; Uranus, the planet of sudden, unexpected changes and brilliant insights, rules Aquarius. In terms of Astro-Yoga, Gemini energy would be beneficial to a student facing a term paper, a writer or researcher in need of information, or a reference librarian. Libra energy would be advantageous for someone in marital counseling, to a dancer or artist, a judge, or even to someone who is decorating his or her home. Aquarian energy would be favorable to a person doing fund-raising or other charitable work, or to anyone who wants his or her work to stand out for its uniqueness.

Energy that works for one situation or need may not be appropriate for another. You're the best judge of the energy you're seeking and in which areas of your life you hope to apply it.

A 30-year-old Cancer woman was preparing to take the state test for her real estate license and felt nervous and uneasy about it because she never did well on standardized tests. We recommended that she do the forehead-to-knees postures daily for two weeks before the tests. These postures relate to Gemini, which, of all the air signs, is aligned most closely with learning and school. Since her natal chart had a predominance of water and earth planets, we also suggested the Libra balance postures and the Aquarian series of shoulder stand postures. The Libra energy would allow her to feel more balanced about the upcoming test and the Aquarian energy would give her a deeper sense of her own uniqueness.

Since she had a Cancer sun, we recommended postures for Capricorn, Cancer's polar opposite. This would not only strengthen the energy from the other earth elements in her chart, but would also increase her ambition to persevere and attain what she wanted.

By the time the day of the test arrived, she brimmed with confidence and certainty that she knew the material. She breezed through the test, passed it with flying colors, and is now selling real estate.

In the following exercise, you're going to do some brainstorming that will help you clarify the air qualities you would like to draw into your life. This, in turn, will enable you to define your intent and will give you a pretty good idea about which areas of your life need the energy.

A young Scorpio woman faced a critical career decision. For years, her parents had planned on her taking over the family funeral business when they retired. She knew the business well and knew that she would make a very comfortable living. Then she was offered a great opportunity in a start-up computer company—but for less money. She felt the offer would be a new beginning for her, but she was reluctant to make such a big change in her life. She also knew that if she took the job, her parents would be devastated because it would mean they would have to sell the funeral business.

To counter the situation, we designed an Astro-Yoga workout that included Libra postures—for balance and harmony in dealing with her family—and Aquarius, since its ruler governs computers. These postures addressed a particular situation in her life at the time and weren't intended to be done any longer than it took for her to work out the particulars. We also recommended that she include the postures for Taurus, Scorpio's polarity, to keep her own dreams fixed and firm in her own mind.

It took longer than she expected to make the transition. An old friend of the family, who her parents trusted, decided to sell his funeral business and buy the one from her parents so he could move back to his hometown. However, the sale of the two businesses and the new owner's move took time. The start-up business held the opening for her, however, and within six months, she was ensconced in her new life.

In the exercise, jot down the situations or issues in your life that you want to work on. Your statement may include more than one thing, but keep your statement simple and concise. The Scorpio woman's statement encompassed several things: *I want to take the new job without leaving Mom and Dad high and dry.*

Read through the attributes for each sign and check those that will help you accomplish your goal and which apply to your situation and issue.

Using the Lists

When you glance through the lists, it's important to think of your life as it is right now. *The present is your point of power.* The present is the place from which you launch the rest of your life.

Brainstorming

Air Sign Attributes

The situations or issues that I would like to work on are: ______________

____

Gemini Attributes

Adaptability ______________

Communication skills ______________

Curiosity ______________

Gathering/disseminating information ______________

Gift of gab ______________

Networker ______________

Sharp perceptions ______________

Versatility ______________

Libra Attributes

Artistic sensitivity ______________

Balance ______________

Cooperation ______________

Diplomatic ______________

Fair-minded ______________

Harmonious ______________

Romantic ______________

Social ______________

Aquarius Attributes

Altruism ______________

Eccentricity/genius ______________

Freedom ______________

Honors individuality ______________

Humanitarian ______________

Idealism ______________

Originality ______________

Radical independence ______________

Areas of my life which pertain to situation or issue

Finances ______________

Personal relationships ______________

General self-improvement ______________

Spirituality ______________

Work/profession ______________

Other notes to myself:

____

____

____

____

____

____

Perhaps your career has taken off, but your personal relationships are floundering. If so, then make sure you've checked off personal relationships in the last section. Maybe you're already adaptable and versatile, but are badly in need of some radical independence. Fine, check it off.

The sign that has the most check marks indicates the specific air energy you should work with to deal with the situations or issues that you jotted at the beginning of the exercise. If no area has more checks than any other, select any of the series of air postures.

Your Body and Air Signs

In astrology, each sign rules a particular part of the body and that body part is considered to be the most vulnerable area for that sign. In planning your workout, consider including postures related to the part of the body your sun sign rules. Gemini, for instance, rules the hands, arms, lungs, and nervous system. If you're a Gemini, consider including the forehead-to-knee postures in your workout and pay special attention to the stretch in your arms. Since Geminis are naturally prone to respiratory ailments, the breathing exercise for air signs is especially important.

If you're an Aquarian (ankles, shins, circulatory system), then when you're doing the shoulder stand series of postures, rotate your ankles in both directions and be aware of the stretching of muscles in your foot as you do so. Inverted postures, such as the shoulder stand, are particularly good for improving circulation.

If you're a Libra (lower back, kidneys, bladder, diaphragm), the balance postures should be done with an awareness of the stretching of muscles in the lower back.

Parts of the Body Ruled by Air Signs

Air Sign	Part of the Body
♊ *Gemini, mutable*	*Hands, arms, lungs, nervous system*
♎ *Libra, cardinal*	*Lower back, kidneys, bladder, diaphragm*
♒ *Aquarius, fixed*	*Ankles, shins, circulatory system*

What's Coming Up

In the next three chapters, we explore the nature of the individual air signs and illustrate the Astro-Yoga techniques that accompany each sign. Take another look at the brainstorming lists in this chapter to see which sign has the most check marks, then turn to the appropriate chapter.

As any seasoned yoga practitioner will tell you, attention and focus are essential when you do the postures. With Astro-Yoga, your full attention is vital because in the intent part of the postures, you're using your body to draw in energy to change or improve your life.

Alternate Nostril Breathing

The breathing exercise for air signs is somewhat more complex than those for the other three elements. While air signs are about intellect and the mental process, alternate nostril breathing works to vitalize the body and balance the two lobes of the brain.

Begin in a seated position with your legs crossed. Bring your right hand up to your nose and fold your fingers toward your palm. Use your thumb to regulate your right nostril and raise your ring finger for your left nostril. Close your right nostril with your thumb and exhale slowly through your left nostril to the count of eight, or eight seconds. Then inhale forcefully through the left nostril to the count of four.

Pinch both nostrils shut and hold to the count of twelve. Exhale through your right nostril, again to the count of eight, keeping the left nostril closed. Inhale deeply to the count of four through the right nostril. Hold to the count of twelve.

Now you've completed one round of alternate nostril breathing. Continue on for three more rounds. Then pause and repeat your intent affirmation, or simply the keywords for the particular air sign that you are working with. Complete another four more rounds of the alternate nostril breathing—with intent.

13

Gemini, the Twins

Theme:
Communication
Keywords:
Adaptability, versatility, mental quickness
May 21–June 21
Ruled by Mercury
Mutable air
Rules lungs, hands, arms, nervous system

Remember the old ad for Doublemint gum? Remember the pair of twins, cute as buttons, and that catchy tune about double your pleasure and double your fun? That energy belongs to Gemini, the twins. What the ad doesn't tell you is that there are two facets to the Gemini energy, each very different.

The first facet might be compared to the little girl in *E.T.*, played by Drew Barrymore. She was the family messenger, quick to sum up a situation and spill the truth as she saw it. Once her brother let her in on his big secret, that there was an alien hidden in his room, she insisted on meeting it. Her curiosity impelled her to go behind that closed door, to flirt with the forbidden, to savor the unknown because it might hold a piece of information, and because, well, she couldn't stand not knowing what was behind the door.

Her brother, the boy who became E.T.'s buddy, was the expression of another facet of Gemini. When he's following the trail of Reese's Pieces into the barn where E.T. is hiding, he is scared to death. We feel his heart pounding, we sweat his sweat, we hope he'll stop and run back into the house. But he keeps moving, steadily and slowly, toward the barn. His curiosity has ignited the torch in his soul. His curiosity is all that exists. He must have *direct experience* of whatever is hidden in the barn and it doesn't matter that he may be putting himself in danger. The sheer brilliance of his curiosity has burned away everything else. In many ways, this is the shadow manifestation of the Gemini twins.

For the typical Gemini, everything in life comes in pairs. One twin wants a house in the country; the other twin insists on living in the city. One twin would like to be married; the other twin enjoys being single. Opposing desires—the heart and the mind perpetually at war.

Rob's cousin is a physicist—science is his middle name. Most of the time, his left brain speaks. He doesn't believe in astrology, in mysticism, or in psychic phenomena. Yet, on a bus bound for Chitzhen Itza, a Mayan ruin in Mexico, he told us a story about meeting Betty and Barney Hill, who recounted their abduction experience that occurred in the early sixties. He had listened to the tapes of their hypnosis sessions, and admitted that he believed *something* had happened to them. Almost in the same breath, he added, "But UFOs? C'mon."

This, too, is Gemini energy. The world must make sense, it has to be logical, C follows B follows A. And yet, mysteries happen. Inexplicable things come up time and again. How does Gemini explain the inconsistencies? She doesn't. She can't and she knows she can't, not unless she does more than scratch the surface of the anomalies.

Jacques Cousteau was a Gemini. It's easy to imagine him underwater, scouring the ocean floor for the pieces of the puzzle. Freud, another Gemini, did the same with the unconscious, and Whitley Streiber does it with aliens. Gemini's questions always start with one of those journalism words: who, what, where, why, how.

For a Gemini, each question strips away another layer that leads to an even deeper mystery. Forget finding a definitive answer. That's not going to happen, and Gemini knows that. But it doesn't matter; she keeps digging, seeking, investigating, asking questions, fitting the pieces together. This is what she is born to do. Her curiosity and lightning quick mind are her greatest resources.

Think of the American West. Aries pioneered it, crossing its vast prairie in wagon trains and on horseback, just to see what was really there. Taurus followed in the footsteps of Aries, cultivating what was pioneered. Taurus built homes, grew crops, and put down roots. Gemini came along behind Taurus and brought in teachers, started newspapers, and networked to keep one town connected to another.

Shadow side? Absolutely. Unanswered phone messages are stacked on Gemini's desk because her marriage is falling apart; because her dog is ailing; because she's so busy fretting about what doesn't work in her life that she can't focus on what *is* working. One moment she commits to lunch on Saturday, the next moment all bets are off; she can't make it because something has come up. She can also be brash, unintentionally blunt, and utterly relentless. She can be the kind of person the rest of us would like to punch in the mouth. But in the end, her friends are the ones who realize she can't be changed, and accept her as she accepts them—as she is.

Gemini's quest is ultimately her challenge as well: to fit the pieces she collects, all that raw data, into a comprehensible whole. To accomplish this, she must draw on the energy of her polarity—Sagittarius, who always seeks the bigger picture first and fills in the details later.

Building a Personalized Workout

As an archetype, Gemini is the communicator who connects people and ideas, collects the facts, and then disseminates them. She tends to understand facts as absolute truths and generally doesn't dig any deeper. By contrast, Sagittarius, Gemini's polar opposite, is the seeker for whom facts and people are primarily vehicles to deeper truths. Geminis usually need deeper truths in their lives and find them by using Sagittarian energy.

So if you're reading this chapter because you're a Gemini, read the chapter on Sagittarius and consider including those postures in your regular yoga workout. If you're reading the Gemini chapter because your brainstorming list indicates you would benefit from Gemini energy, read through the postures that follow this section. Do them the first time to acquaint yourself with them. Notice how you feel physically and emotionally as you go through the series. Does your body feel good? Does it ache? Do you sense any pockets of emotional resistance in yourself? If so, explore the resistance. Try to determine why you feel that way.

When you go through the postures the second time, do so with *intent*. This involves both an affirmation and a visualization.

Intent affirmation: *I now pull in versatility, mental quickness, and clarity of perception.*

Create an affirmation that fits the Gemini qualities you're seeking. Play around with the wording, but keep it simple and clear.

Intent visualization: While you're saying your affirmation, visualize the end result of the situation or issue with which you're working. If, for example, you're trying to develop your communication skills in preparation for an upcoming presentation, then see yourself speaking with utter ease. See your idea being accepted and implemented. Put feeling behind it; see the people to whom you're presenting the idea or project; see the walls and the arrangement of furniture in the room. The more vivid the visualization, the greater your chance of success.

Don't concern yourself with *how* it's going to come about. Simply trust that things will unfold to your greatest benefit, without harming anyone else.

Forehead-to-Knee Series

The forehead encases the frontal lobe of the brain and the knee is a point of flexibility. When the two body parts touch, they symbolize the nature of the air sign Gemini, whose energy focuses on ideas, communication, versatility, and adaptability. From a physical standpoint, the postures improve flexibility and stretch your hamstring and hip muscles.

Corpse Position

The **corpse position** is just like it sounds: lay on your back, corpselike, and completely relaxed. Let go of any tension in your neck, shoulders, back, or hips. Breathe gently in and out through your nose and focus on your breath for at least thirty seconds.

Water Wheel

When you're relaxed and ready to continue, pick up your feet and bring your knees to your chest. Then slowly raise your legs above your hips, forming an L with your body. Keep your legs straight, and lower them gently down. Just before your heels touch the floor, bend your knees into your chest again, and continue around in the **water wheel**. After three or four revolutions, reverse directions and repeat the movement. When you are finished, let your feet turn out, relaxing the hips.

Knee-Down Twist

Next, lift up your right knee and hook your big toe underneath your left thigh. Extend your right arm straight out from the shoulder and turn your head to the right. Now let your raised knee sink down toward the floor on the left side of your body. Keep your right shoulder down as you enter the **knee-down twist** (Figure 13-1). You can also place your left hand on the outside of your bent knee, allowing it to sink closer to the floor. Hold for five or six breaths. Keep your muscles relaxed and, if your knee

Figure 13-1 Knee-Down Twist

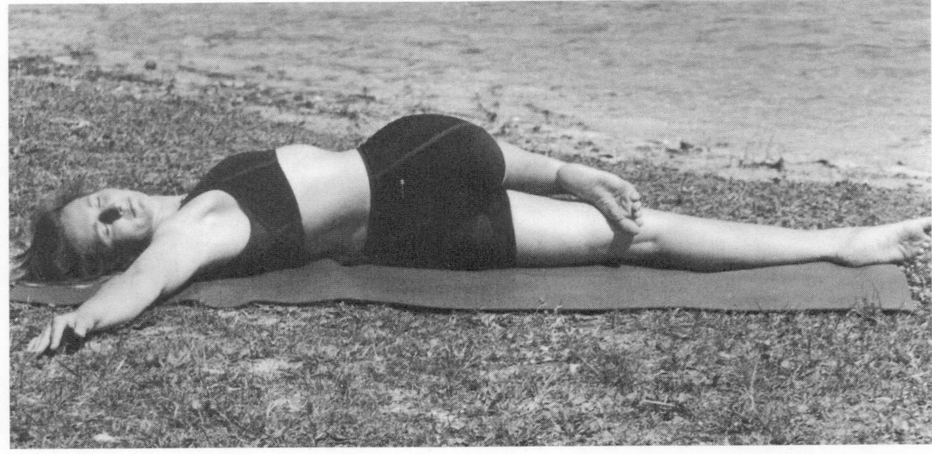

Figure 13-2 Thigh-to-Chest

Figure 13-3 Reclining Half-Lotus

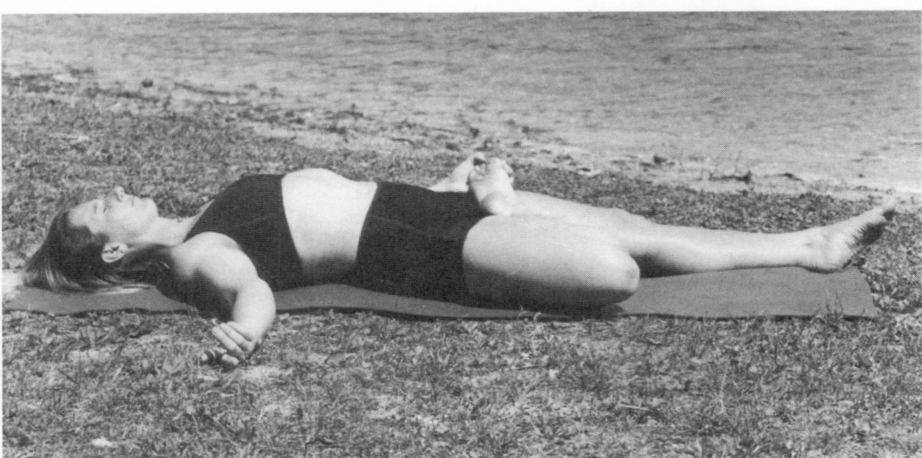

doesn't reach the floor, be careful not to overextend the stretch. With practice, the knee will sink farther down.

Reclining Half-Lotus

Raise your knee back up and clasp your hands below the knee in the **thigh-to-chest** pose (Figure 13-2). At the same time, push out through your left heel. Hold for two or three breaths, then reach for your right ankle with your left hand. Pull your ankle onto your thigh and let your knee drop down as you open your hip in the **reclining half-lotus** (Figure 13-3). Hold for at least three breaths. Anyone with knee problems should use caution when entering this position. The same is true for the following pose.

Heel-to-Hip Stretch

For the **heel-to-hip stretch**, lift your knee back up and this time clasp your right ankle with your right hand. Pull your heel toward the outside of the hip, then let the knee drop down next to the opposite knee. If you can flatten the top of your foot against the mat, you can release your hand (Figure 13-4). Hold the position for another three breaths or more.

Repeat the knee-down twist, reclining half-lotus, and heel-to-hip poses with your left leg.

Figure 13-4 Heel-to-Hip Stretch

Forehead-to-Knee Posture

Next, bring your right thigh to your chest again, clasping your hands below the knee. Hold for at least three breaths, then walk your hands up your leg. Clasp onto your calf, ankle, or foot, straightening your leg and simultaneously raising your forehead to your knee (Figure 13-5). Hold the **forehead-to-knee** posture for five or six breaths.

Drop your head back to the mat and stretch a little deeper (Figure 13-6). Again hold for five or six breaths, then slowly lower your leg to the floor. Raise your left knee to your chest and repeat the forehead-to-knee pose.

Figure 13-5 Forehead-to-Knee Position One

Figure 13-6 Forehead-to-Knee Position Two

Figure 13-7 Bicycle Crunches

Bicycle Crunches

Before moving to the intent phase, you can finish the series with several **bicycle crunches**, where you again bring the forehead to your knee. This time, however, clasp your hands behind your head and raise your bent knee to your forehead (Figure 13-7). Straighten your leg slowly and bend your left knee to your forehead. Go back and forth for at least five repetitions on either side. Stay at the same pace, moving in slow motion.

After you've completed form, move to the intent phase of the Gemini postures. Work with the postures and draw in the energy of the air sign using your keywords—*adaptable*, *versatile*, *mental quickness*. Where in your life do you need better communication, to be more adaptable, or more versatile? Focus on bringing the energy into those areas of your life.

Variations

In place of bicycle crunches, you can try the **scissors**. Keep your leg straight as you bring your forehead to your knee. Like the bicycle crunches, your hands are clasped behind the head. Move slowly while alternating legs (Figure 13-8).

For a more challenging variation of the knee-down twist, clasp your big toe with your first two fingers, then straighten your

Figure 13-8 Scissors

leg as best you can. Now slowly lower the leg to the right, directly out from your hip. Keep the left buttock on the mat. When you reach the maximum stretch, hold the extended-leg twist for three breaths (Figure 13-9). Raise your leg up again, above your body, and bring your forehead to your knee for three more breaths.

Switch hands, taking the big toe with the first two fingers of your left hand. Lower your leg to the left, toward the floor, and roll onto your left hip, into position two of the extended-leg twist (Figure 13-10). Hold for three breaths. Raise the leg up again, bring your forehead to your knee, and hold for three breaths. Slowly lower the leg to the floor. Switch legs and repeat the postures.

Rather than replacing the knee-down twist with these two postures, you can add them into your workout as an option. If you are unable to straighten your leg in performing the two related postures, practice them with a bent knee.

Alternate Nostril Breathing

After completing the intent round of the series, come into a seated position for the breathing exercise related to the air signs. See Chapter 12.

Figure 13-9 Extended-Leg Twist Position One

Figure 13-10 Extended-Leg Twist Position Two

14

Libra, the Scales

Theme:
Exploring partnerships
Keywords:
Balance, cooperation, harmony
September 23–October 22
Ruled by Venus
Cardinal air
Rules lower back, kidneys, bladder, diaphragm

Take a prism. Turn it slowly in the sunlight, so each facet is clearly revealed. That's how Libra's perception works. He sees every side of an issue or situation. It's his gift, but can also be his curse, depending on how he applies it.

This perceptual ability makes him an excellent diplomat, judge, or attorney. If he's involved in the arts, his unusual perceptions result in works of art that are often extraordinary. Actress Susan Sarandon, for instance, has played everything from a woman seduced by a vampire in *The Hunger* to a nun in *Dead Man Walking*, for which she won an Oscar. In whatever role she plays, her extraordinary Libran energy brings the character to life.

Where Aries is brash and bold, Libra energy is yin and intuitive, softer around the edges. Aries is the independent loner, but Libra flourishes in intimate relationships. In fact, relationships are the field on which Libra's perceptions focus. Even when he's very young, this tendency is evident.

He is polite, amiable, and socially skillful. He can also be so charming and diplomatic that he's often mistaken for a pushover, a big mistake on the part of the person who comes to such a conclusion. Libra uses his diplomacy and intelligence to get what he wants.

Libra usually deplores vulgarity and crudeness in any form. This runs true even in his taste for music, art, and films. Forget heavy metal. Forget Dali and *Natural Born Killers*. He'll take Beethoven, Matisse, and *Field of Dreams*. Even though Libra is considered to be an artistic sign, it doesn't mean that all Librans are artists. Yet the arts, in its various forms, frequently play an important role in his life. He may be a collector of art and music, or a patron of the arts. He may encourage artistic or musical expression in others, or it may be that he visits museums the way other people frequent bookstores or shopping malls.

Since both Libra and Taurus are ruled by Venus, it's no surprise that they both need harmony in their lives. The difference is that when Taurus doesn't have it, she goes off by herself to create peace from nature and solitude; Libra simply comes unglued. He can't unplug from other people the way Taurus can. He can't tell his significant other to hit the road, his boss to back off, his grown son to move out. To take any of those actions would be to descend into vulgarity or crassness. *It would be mean*. Besides, his curse is that he understands why his significant other feels as hostile as she does. He understands why his boss is so dictatorial. He understands why his son is having problems. He sees their side.

To restore peace and harmony in his life, he bends over backward to make things better for everyone else. He becomes a mediator in his own life, doing whatever he can to keep the peace, but at the expense of his own needs. Or, because he can't bring himself to end his relationship or to walk away from his job, he creates a secret life. This is usually where Libra gets into trouble because he quickly discovers that maintaining two lives is more complicated than dealing with one.

When Libra is unfaithful, it's often because he can't stand the thought of a nasty confrontation that will hurt the other person. He can't stand the thought of a confrontation, period. It seems easier to just let things coast along and hope the other person will end the relationship. This tendency contributes to Libra's reputation as a procrastinator or as lazy, which isn't the case at all. It's just that when a decision involves confrontation, he would rather not go that route.

This shadow side of Libra can be mitigated by pulling in energy from Aries, Libra's polar opposite. Aries rarely avoids confrontation, and, since he's more independent, he usually doesn't get himself into duplicitous situations. Where Libra waffles, Aries makes snap decisions. They may not always be the right decisions, but right or wrong, Aries acts.

The irony, of course, is that balance, which Libra represents, is the most difficult state for a Libra individual to attain and maintain. Part of the problem is that Libra is a true romantic, one of those people who is in love with love. He needs moonlight, poetry, ocean breezes. In his constant efforts to beautify his notions of love, he re-creates his relationships to match those notions. When the reality fails to live up to his expectations, disharmony erupts in his life and the entire cycle starts over.

The challenge for Libra is to create harmony and balance in his life without compromising to the point where his own needs are subsumed. It's a tall order for Libra and, sooner or later, one he must fulfill.

Building a Personalized Workout

For Libras reading this section, turn to the Aries chapter and read through the postures. Consider including them in your regular workout.

If you're reading the Libra chapter because your brainstorming checklist suggests that you need Libra energy in your life, then read through the balance postures. When you do them for the first time, be aware of how your body feels. Can you relax into the balance postures or are you tense or uneasy? Also pay attention to how you feel emotionally. Bringing conscious awareness to the postures is the first step in using your body as a vehicle for transformation. When you do the postures a second time, do them with *intent.*

Intent affirmation: *I draw harmony, balance, and artistic sensibilities into my life.*

The affirmation is the first part of doing the postures with intent. Create an affirmation that includes whatever qualities you're trying to pull into your life. Keep it simple and in the present tense. This affirmation will change as your needs and goals change, so play around with the wording to fit the needs you have now.

Intent visualization: The secret to creating a visualization that works is to make it vivid and not to worry about the little details. In other words, if you're trying to bring a relationship into balance, visualize the end result—not how you're going to get there.

The visualization, like the affirmation, will change as your needs and goals change. Once your relationship is brought into balance, for instance, you may discover that you want to bring balance into your professional life. Word the affirmation and change the visualization accordingly.

The Balance Series

No other sign of the zodiac fits the balance series as well as the air sign Libra, which is symbolized by a balance scale. In all the Libra postures, with the exception of the crow, you will balance on one foot. Although balance is the essence of the postures, some of them also call for strength and endurance.

If you have difficulty with balance postures, practice them near a chair or wall. That way you can get used to standing on one foot without concern for staying balanced more than a few seconds. Hold the postures for at least fifteen seconds. Increase to thirty seconds, then a minute. You may want to start with only two or three postures in this series and gradually work up to a full set of five or six. We'll begin with the easiest and work toward the more strenuous postures.

After you've completed a set of the postures on each foot, move from form to intent using your keywords—*balance, harmony, cooperation, partnership*. You may want to vary some of the postures for your intent set, focusing on the ones that you have mastered. That way you'll be more centered on using your intent than trying to maintain your balance.

Balance Warm-Up

Stand with your feet about six inches apart. Keeping both legs straight, lift your right leg a few inches off the floor in front of you. Point your toes and hold for about fifteen seconds. Without touching your foot to the floor, move your leg to the right so that it's in line with your shoulders. Flex your foot, pushing through the heel. After another fifteen seconds, swing the leg back, point your toes, and hold. Switch legs and repeat these balance poses.

Tree Posture

This balance posture is one of the most common in yoga classes, as it challenges your flexibility and balance. Bring your weight to your left foot and lift your right heel to your ankle just touching your toes to the mat. Now bring your palms to your chest. This is the easiest form of the **tree**.

If that presents little or no challenge, raise your foot to your calf, your knee, or your thigh (Figure 14-1). Alternately, you can bring your foot to the front of your left thigh. If you're flexible, see if you can bring your heel to the outside of your left hip. Now bring your palms to your chest and hold for a few breaths. If you're well rooted, straighten your arms up overhead, clasping your fingers together and pointing your index fingers (Figure 14-2).

Figure 14-1 Tree Posture One

Figure 14-2 Tree Posture Two

Lower your arms to your sternum again and release your foot. Repeat with the left foot.

Standing Knee-to-Chest

A simple balance posture that requires minimal stretching, the **standing knee-to-chest** pose can serve as a warm-up for the tree or the extended-leg postures. From the mountain pose, lift your right knee and clasp your hands below it. Pull your thigh toward your belly. Keep your back straight and your shoulders back (Figure 14-3). See if you can hold this posture for a full minute, then switch legs.

Figure 14-3 Standing Knee-to-Chest

Figure 14-4 Bowing to Leg

Bowing to Leg

Once you've mastered the knee-to-chest pose, the next step is to reach for the bottom of your foot with both hands as you bend chest to thigh in the **bowing to leg** pose. Then, extend your leg forward. Ideally, you maintain your hold on your foot. If that's too difficult, grasp your ankle or calf. Fold your chest and forehead to your leg (Figure 14-4). Hold for three or four breaths, then switch legs.

Standing Extended Leg

A somewhat more challenging posture than the previous one, the **standing extended leg** stretches the hamstring while you maintain your balance and poise. Bend your right knee to your chest and hook your first two fingers around your big toe. Standing as

Figure 14-5 Standing Extended Leg A

Figure 14-6 Standing Extended Leg B

upright as possible, extend your leg in front of you (Figure 14-5). If you are unable to straighten your leg without leaning forward, keep your leg bent and stand erect.

Alternately, extend your leg to the right, opening up your hip (Figure 14-6). Again, if you can't straighten your leg, keep your knee bent in order to maintain your upright stance. Neither option is necessarily more difficult than the other. Some yoga students experience more difficulty extending the leg to the side than forward, but others find the opposite is true. Hold the posture for three or four breaths, then switch legs.

The Eagle

Start the **eagle** pose by raising your arms to shoulder level and bringing your left elbow inside your right elbow. Then wrap your right arm around your left and try to bring the palms of your hands together. If you can't stretch far enough, hook your left thumb against the fingers of your right hand. That's the half-eagle. Now, bring the back of your right knee over your left knee and hook your right foot around your left calf (Figure 14-7). If you want to go further, bend your knees and raise your arms.

The Raindancer

This balance posture combines balance, form, and grace. While standing, raise your right foot behind you, and clasp your foot with your right hand. Keep your knees close together. Once you are firmly established in this position, simultaneously raise your right foot behind you and extend your left arm in front of you, gracefully arching your back as you look forward (Figure 14-8).

Make sure that your raised knee doesn't splay out to the side. For added leverage, clasp the inside of your foot by rotating

Figure 14-7 The Eagle

Figure 14-8 The Raindancer

your hand in a clockwise motion. That way your shoulder opens up rather than turns inward, allowing you to extend further. Hold the **raindancer** for up to thirty seconds. Focus on your breath to help maintain your stability. Switch legs and repeat.

Airplane

Start in the lunge posture with your bent right knee over the ankle, your left leg extended, and your hands on the mat. Rest your chest on your thigh. Raise your arms out to the sides, parallel with the floor, and hold for five or six breaths. Next, lean forward and lift your left leg parallel to the mat (Figure 14-9). In **airplane** pose, you can either look down or straight ahead, raising your chest higher. Hold for three or four breaths, then switch sides.

Alternately, you can reach forward and straighten your supporting leg (Figure 14-10). Hold for another three or four breaths. Switch legs.

Figure 14-9 Airplane

Figure 14-10 Airplane Variation

Crow

For **crow**, one of the more challenging balance postures, you start from a squatting position with your arms between your knees. Raise up onto your toes. Then raise one leg and bring the shin onto your upper arm. Bring the other leg into the same position and find your balance (Figure 14-11). If that's too much, work with just one leg raised at a time. Eventually, you'll be able to briefly lift the second leg off the mat. Hold the position for three or four breaths. Repeat and try to hold for longer.

Extended-Leg Squat

Again begin from a squat. This time keep your feet flat and place your fingertips on the mat below your hips. Now extend your left leg and point your toes (Figure 14-12). Once you're stable, bring your palms to your chest (Figure 14-13). You can also try

Figure 14-11 The Crow

Figure 14-12 Extended-Leg Squat

the **extended-leg squat** on your toes or out to the side, as shown on page 183. Hold for five or six breaths, then switch legs.

Squatting Tree

Start from the standing tree posture with your palms at your chest and your right foot on your thigh. Then sink down into a deep squat for **squatting tree** (Figure 14-14). If you have tight hips, you may only get part of the way down before the stretch becomes too intense. Go as far as is comfortable, while experiencing the stretch, and hold for three or four breaths. Switch legs.

Variations

Once you've gotten familiar with these postures, you can work on combining them. Start with the knee-to-chest pose with your right leg. Then, after holding for at least three breaths, reach for your big toe with your first two fingers and extend your leg in front of you. After several more breaths, swing your leg to the right and hold again. Bring your leg back in front of you and reach for your

Figure 14-13 Modified Extended-Leg Squat

Figure 14-14 Squatting Tree

ankle with both hands and bow to your leg. Hold for at least three breaths, then release, and stand erect while holding your leg out in front of you with your hands on your hips. After a few breaths, lower the leg to the floor, and repeat with the other leg.

Another combination starts with the tree posture. Then, without lowering your foot to the floor, go into the raindancer. After several breaths, release and extend the leg in front of you, reach for your ankle with both hands, and bow to the leg. Release and switch legs.

These are just a few of the many balance postures and variations. If you know others from yoga classes you've taken, you can work your favorite ones into your Libra routine.

Alternate Nostril Breathing

After completing the intent round of the series, sit down in a cross-legged position for the breathing exercise related to the air signs. See Chapter 12 for an explanation of alternate nostril breathing.

15

Aquarius, the Water Bearer

Theme:
Creating alternatives
Keywords:
Freedom, individuality, vision
January 20–February 18
Ruled by Uranus
Fixed air
Rules throat, shins, and circulatory system

Individual freedom: that's the song of Aquarian energy. The individual is paramount because it's only through individuals that the human collective can be changed. In the Aquarian scheme of things, mass movements begin with a single, burning thought in the mind of a single individual. But to have that single burning thought, all people must be free to express the truth as they see it—even when it goes against mainstream beliefs. No sign is better equipped to bust old paradigms and to usher in new ones. It's the Aquarian destiny, a predilection wired into their very cells.

But forget revolutions for a moment; forget mass movements. How is this particular pattern of energy manifested in daily life? In exactly the same way that it manifests itself in the larger sense. The Aquarian individual is an eccentric, original thinker. Tell her the sky is blue and she nods as if in agreement, but then investigates the issue on her own. If she decides you're wrong, that the sky is actually yellow, not blue, then nothing can shake her from what her own perceptions tell her. Like Sagittarius, she's after the truth, but the difference is that Aquarius is looking for *her* truth, which nearly always runs counter to the truth held by other people. But again, this is her genius.

For Aquarius, romance and love are primarily mental qualities. To win her heart, you must seduce her mind, and allow her the freedom her nature demands. If you do this, it's unlikely that she'll ever betray you. This holds true in every area of her life. The New Hampshire motto, in fact, fits Aquarius—Live free or die.

Aquarius is a genuinely altruistic sign. She can't stand to see anyone suffering or in pain. Images from the nightly news about famine in Ethiopia, human rights abuses, wars around the globe—nothing stirs her compassion more quickly or deeply. She's likely to whip out her checkbook for a donation or volunteer her services on the spot.

She's also one of the most genuinely tolerant signs in the zodiac, respectful of everyone's beliefs and spiritual creeds. She doesn't recognize the boundaries that divide most of humanity—differences in race, culture, religion, and financial status. She can talk to a janitor just as easily as she can converse with a CEO. She instinctively understands that these differences are what make each of us unique and, because of that understanding, is incapable of passing judgment on whether something is right or wrong for someone else.

But when it comes to her own beliefs and opinions, she can be as stubborn as Taurus, another fixed sign. Once she decides what is right for her, not much will change her mind. The danger is that she can become stuck in her beliefs and remain there even after society has caught up to her. Then she's in danger of becoming what she has eschewed—a conformist whose individuality is merely a shadow darting across the lawn at dusk.

To mitigate this shadow side of Aquarius, it's necessary for her to draw on the energy of Leo, her polar opposite. Leo is emotional where Aquarius is detached. Leo lives from the heart,

Aquarius from the mind. The idea here is fairly straightforward: merge heart and mind, left brain and right, and the result may be what Aquarius loves best—a completely new and unique way of being.

Astrologers continue to disagree on when the Aquarian Age began. But regardless of its exact beginning, this age promises to be unlike any other. The Aquarian energy is already dissolving paradigms in medicine and health care, quantum physics, education, politics, and access to information. Nothing will remain untouched. What betters life for one, betters life for all. We are interconnected; life is a living, breathing hologram. That's the Aquarian axiom.

Even though Aquarius knows who she is and what she's about, her challenge is to make the leap from intellectual compassion to compassion that comes from the heart. Until she makes that leap, she encounters barriers and restrictions and attracts circumstances that challenge her individuality and her freedom. At some point, she must take the leap of faith that comes straight from the heart rather than the mind.

Building a Personalized Workout

Mind and heart, intellect and feelings: that's the fulcrum of the Aquarius/Leo polarity. So if you're reading Chapter 15 because you're an Aquarius, turn to Chapter 6 and read the Leo postures. It would be a good idea to include those postures in your regular workout.

If you're reading this chapter because the brainstorming activity suggests a need for Aquarian energy, then read through the shoulder stand/bridge series of postures. Your first time through, do the postures primarily to determine their ease or difficulty for you. Do you feel any tightness in your body as you're doing them? Does anything hurt? How do you feel emotionally? Are you bored or invigorated? Explore any negative feelings or thoughts you might have and try to determine their source.

One young man, a Virgo, found that he was irritable during the shoulder stand series. When he explored the feeling, he realized the problem was his inability to come fully upright in the full shoulder stand, and to a Virgo, anything less than perfection just isn't acceptable. Once he understood that perfection of the postures isn't the point, he was able to relax into a modified version of the shoulder stand and actually come to enjoy the posture.

Your second time through the postures should be done with *intent*.

Intent affirmation: *I now draw in originality and independence*. When creating an affirmation, use words that describe the specific qualities you're trying to pull in. Play around with it until it feels right and keep it simple and direct.

Intent visualization: As you're saying your affirmation, visualize the end result of the situation or issue with which you're working. If, for instance, you're seeking personal freedom in your professional life in order to start your own business, visualize yourself with the business already underway. Don't concern yourself with *how* it's going to come about. Don't try to connect the dots in the visualization; simply focus on the end result and trust that things will unfold to your greatest benefit, without harming anyone else.

The Shoulder Stand/ Bridge Series

When your feet are above your head, as in the shoulder stand series, you look at the world from a different perspective. That's the essence of Aquarian energy. Aquarius is also a bridge between new and old, and therefore, the bridge postures symbolize the transition from past to future.

The shoulder stand invigorates the entire body. In fact, the Sanskrit name for the posture, *savangasana*, literally means, "all parts pose." In particular, you stretch the neck and upper spine. Like all inverted postures, it stimulates the thyroid and pituitary glands, which control sexual energies. It reverses the flow of blood as well as the direction of gravity on the body, allowing the heart to rest and bringing more blood to the brain.

The bridge postures, which are counter poses to the shoulder stand, strengthen the lower back, neck, and shoulder muscles. The poses improve flexibility of the spine and wrists and also stretch the abdominal muscles.

The series, like the ones for Gemini and Pisces, begins in the easiest of all yoga postures, the corpse pose, in which you simply lie on your back, relax, and quiet your mind.

Extended L-Posture

When you are ready to begin, quiet your mind and move into the L-posture, with your legs raised above your hips. Place your palms down, tense your abdominal muscles, and lift your tailbone an inch or two off the floor. Press your palms into the mat (Figure 15-1). Hold for two or three breaths. The **extended L-posture** is a subtle movement, one that tenses the abdominal muscles and prepares you for the shoulder stand.

Figure 15-1 Extended L-Posture

Figure 15-2 Modified Shoulder Stand

Figure 15-3 Shoulder Stand

Shoulder Stand

Bend your knees into your chest, placing your hands on your knees. Make small circles one way, then the other, as you prepare for the shoulder stand. Come back into the L-pose, but this time extend your legs beyond your head and lift your back off the floor. Brace your lower back with your hands to enter a modified shoulder stand (Figure 15-2). Hold for at least five or six breaths.

If this posture causes too much strain on your back or neck, bend your knees into your chest. If you feel any pain related to past neck or back injuries, come down from the posture and move on to the rest of the series. If not, come up into the full **shoulder stand** by raising your feet above your shoulders (Figure 15-3). Hold for another five or six breaths.

Figure 15-4 The Plow

The Plow

Next, stretch your feet back behind you and continue down into the **plow**, ideally touching your toes to the mat behind you. Clasp your hands together and push your wrists toward the mat (Figure 15-4). Hold for three or four breaths.

Slowly lower down, keeping your thighs close to your chest. Place your palms flat against the mat to steady yourself and control your descent. As your hips come down, bring your legs away from your upper body and gently lower them to the mat. Take three or four breaths in the corpse position.

Pelvic Tilt

From corpse position, raise your knees, keeping your feet flat and about six to twelve inches apart. Arch your back slightly, then lower it down. Arch again, a little higher this time, and come down. As you go up again, start to bring your shoulder blades closer together. Lower your body down and repeat. The next time you lower your back down, raise your hips a couple of inches off the mat and push the middle of your back down. Lower down, arch your back again, then sink back down. Continue the movement, alternately arching your back and raising your hips in the **pelvic tilt**. It's a subtle movement and an excellent warm-up for the next posture.

The Bridge

Raise your hips up so that they are aligned with your knees and shoulders. Clasp your hands beneath you and push your hips up into the **bridge**. Try to keep your knees from moving apart (Figure 15-5A). Hold for up to five or six breaths. Release and sink down. Come up again after a short break. Either go into the same posture, or brace your lower back with your hands and arch your back in position two of the bridge (Figure 15-5B). Hold for the same number of breaths, then release.

Come up for the third time into either of the first two bridge postures, or walk your feet in a little closer and clasp your ankles as you arch your back. Make sure that your heels touch the mat, and try to bring your knees together (Figure 15-5C). Hold for at least five or six breaths before coming down.

Relax into the corpse for a minute before you go into the intent phase of the Aquarius workout. You might take this time to consider what aspect of your life can use the energy of Aquarius. Are you working on a project that requires originality? Do you feel restricted or limited in some respect and in need of more freedom? Do you have a vision you want to fulfill or would you want to create a vision for your life? Would you somehow like to work to better mankind or commit yourself to a cause? Now repeat the series with intent.

Variations

From the plow position, raise one leg and point your toes. Lower the leg down and repeat two or three more times, then switch legs (Figure 15-6). If you are flexible, you can replace one or more of the bridge poses with the **wheel**. Place your palms down beneath the shoulders, lift your hips, and arch your back. Straighten your arms (Figure 15-7) and hold for five or six breaths.

Figure 15-5A The Bridge Position One

Figure 15-5B The Bridge Position Two

Figure 15-5C The Bridge Position Three

Figure 15-6 ***Raised Leg Plow***

Figure 15-7 The Wheel

Alternate Nostril Breathing

After completing the intent round of the series, sit up and cross your legs in preparation for the breathing exercise related to the air signs. See Chapter 12 for details on alternate nostril breathing.

WATER

16

Water: Emotions and Intuition

Frank Herbert's classic science fiction novel, *Dune*, depicts a world that is mostly desert. It's impossible to read the book or see the movie without feeling a terrible dryness in your mouth, a grittiness on your skin, and a yearning in your heart for water. Water to drink, to swim in, to bathe in. You start craving the sound of rain, the sight of the ocean, the coolness of a mountain stream. Nothing stirs an appreciation of water faster than the possibility of being without it.

There are inner seas as well. For the nine months of our gestation, we live like little fish in the noisy silence of embryonic waters. Our blood is one of the inner seas. So are our emotions and intuition. Our deepest inner sea is the collective unconscious, a level of mind/spirit that unites us all.

The idea here, of course, is that water doesn't simply represent the water that we can see. In astrology, water also symbolizes the feelings and instincts that we can't see, our dreams and fantasies, our mystical and inexplicable experiences, our deepest beliefs and our collective selves.

Fire signs experience life primarily through action; earth signs through endurance and stability; air signs through intellect; and water signs through emotions. They literally *feel* their way through everything. Water signs tend to be naturally intuitive, with their intuition usually clustered around particular areas of their life. Cancer, for example, is most likely to be intuitive when it comes to home and family. Scorpio's intuitive domain centers around issues that involve death, metaphysics, joint resources, sexuality, anything strange or unknown. For Pisces, intuition is most deeply connected to the unconscious—dreams, the collective mind, the mystical and mysterious. These are only broad generalizations, but good starting points for understanding how water signs perceive the world and themselves.

Just as each water sign has a different intuitive approach, so does each sign have a different emotional approach. Cancer's strategy is to evade emotional confrontation by sidestepping the issue, moving like the crab that symbolizes it. Scorpio's emotions run very deep and she is intensely passionate about everything she loves. But she is careful not to show it unless she trusts you. For Pisces, all of life is subjective and emotions move through her with the ebb and flow of tides.

The planets that rule each of the water signs set the tone for the energy of that sign. The moon, Cancer's ruler, is the fastest moving, with eight distinct phases each month. It rules ocean tides, blood tides, our unconscious motives, our capacity to nurture, and in a chart, it represents the mother figure or her equivalent. So Cancerian energy is ever changing, nurturing, intuitive, and primarily internal and imaginative. In terms of Astro-Yoga, you might want to pull in Cancer's energy if you were looking for a new house or place to live, trying to get pregnant, or attempting anything that needed to be nurtured.

Pluto, the most distant planet in our solar system and one of the most powerful in astrology, rules Scorpio. This tiny swirl of frozen gases is considered a transpersonal planet. Its movement is so slow that it affects not only individuals, but entire generations. In mythology, Pluto ruled the underworld—the place no one liked to talk about. And that place is where Scorpio lives and breathes. Whatever Scorpio tackles is either conquered—or destroyed. Transformation occurs at the most fundamental and profound levels. There's a certain spiritual risk to pulling in the energy of Scorpio precisely because its power is so seductive.

In daily life, you might draw Scorpio's energy if you're facing dramatic situations and issues and want them changed or resolved once and for all. You might call on this energy to deepen your sexual relationship with the person you love, to get a business loan or mortgage, to deepen your intuitive awareness, or to face life-and-death situations. You should not, however, be frivolous with this energy.

Then there's Pisces, ruled by Neptune, the planet of illusions. Neptune dissolves barriers; that's the long and short of it. And for Pisces, the barrier between the conscious and unconscious mind is little more than a thin veil. So if you're in therapy, you might want to draw in the energy of Pisces. If you're doing dream work or are involved in a creative project that demands imagination, Piscean energy might deepen the process.

An 18-year-old Libra woman, a freshman in college, was supposed to design an invention for her science class. She had procrastinated on getting started because she didn't know where to begin. We recommended doing the upward boat/incline plane series (Pisces) with intent to deepen her imagination, and suggested that she pay close attention to her dreams for clues. Since she was a Libra, we also recommended that she include the warrior postures (Aries, Libra's polarity) in her regular workout. Aries energy would counterbalance Libra's inertia and move her in new, pioneering directions.

With her project in mind, she also went through the brainstorming lists. Aquarius—innovative and original thinking—came out way ahead, so she also included the shoulder stand postures in her workout. Within two weeks, she'd broken through her inertia and was busy on her invention.

The following exercise is a brainstorming list to help you decide if you need water energy in your life, and if so, which kind. The list will help you define your intent and should give you a clear idea about which area of your life needs the energy. You also will jot down the situations or issues that you would like to work on. Your statement can include more than one situation or issue, but keep the wording simple. The woman mentioned above came up with: *I want to invent something that will get me an A in science for this semester.*

Brainstorming

Water Sign Attributes

The situations or issues that I would like to work on are: ______

______

Cancer Attributes

Comfort ______ Mothering ______

Compassion ______ Nurture ______

Empathy ______ Protect ______

Healing ______ Tenderness ______

Scorpio Attributes

Passion ______ Release ______

Piercing perception ______ Renew ______

Power ______ Sexuality ______

Psychic ability ______ Transformation ______

Pisces Attributes

Compassion ______ Inspired creativity ______

Connections to higher mind ______ Intuition ______

Deeper states of consciousness ______ Mysticism ______

Imagination ______ Spiritual insights ______

Areas of my life which pertain to situation or issue

Finances ______ Spirituality ______

Personal relationships ______ Work/profession ______

General self-improvement ______

Other notes to myself:

______

______

______

______

______

Using the Lists

The lists focus on the most positive traits of each sign. You probably already possess some of these traits, but perhaps don't apply them to the areas of your life where you need them the most. As you glance through the lists, think of your life as it is in this instant and work from there. The present—not the past—is your point of power. Forget mistakes or errors in judgment that you've made in the past. Forget who you have been or not been. None of that matters. You're using the present as a launching point for the rest of your life.

If you've checked off more than two areas that pertain to the issue or situation you want to work on, whittle the list down to the most pressing area. This can be a tricky thing to do because the areas of our lives overlap and intersect. But the idea here is to focus. If you try to work on too many areas at once, your workout and your energy will be scattered.

The sign that has the most check marks under it is the specific water energy you should work with. If no area has more checks than any other, choose any of the series of water sign postures.

Your Body and Water Signs

Each sign rules certain parts of the body and those parts are considered to be the most vulnerable. In designing your personal workout, you may want to periodically include postures for your own sun sign. If you're a Cancer, for instance, you would do the moon salutation postures and pay special attention to the stretching of the muscles through your stomach, which Cancer rules.

For Scorpio, which rules the sexual organs, rectum, and reproductive system, the camel/abdominal stretch series of postures should be done with an awareness of how the internal muscles feel. For Pisces, which rules the feet and lymphatic system, the various postures should be done with awareness focused on those parts of the body.

Parts of the Body Ruled by Water Signs

Water Sign	Part of the Body
♋ Cancer, cardinal	Breasts, stomach, digestive system
♏ Scorpio, fixed	Sexual organs, rectum, reproductive system
♓ Pisces, mutable	Feet and lymphatic system

What's Coming Up

The next three chapters explore each of the three water signs and the Astro-Yoga postures that go along with them. Glance over your brainstorming lists in this chapter, and then turn to the right chapter. Remember to go through the postures first before attempting to use your intent.

There are two steps to the intent part of the equation: an affirmation and a visualization. We include suggestions for both for each sign, but this is your workout, so you can design the affirmation and visualization to fit your needs and goals. Either before you begin the intent portion of your workout with the water sign or signs, or after completing the series, you can move your focus to your breath for another exercise that draws on the energy of the water signs. Here's how.

The Wave Breath

This breathing exercise, like a smooth ocean wave, rolls in and then out. The wave breath begins in the same movement as the diaphragmatic breathing exercise related to the earth signs. You lie on your back and push up your belly as you inhale. But now instead of immediately releasing the breath, you roll the bubble of air like a wave up to the middle chest, and then to the upper chest. The wave then rolls out as you move the bubble of air back down toward the belly. Exhale, releasing your breath and allowing the belly to sink down toward the spine. The wave dissipates, but then another one begins to rise.

Continue with the breath for a minute or two. Pause. Consider the keywords for the water sign you are working with or your personal affirmation. Then begin again, using your intent, drawing in the energy for at least one minute.

17

Cancer, the Crab

Theme:
Seeking security
Keywords:
Caring, comforting, nurturing
June 22–July 22
Cardinal water
Ruled by the moon
Rules breasts, stomach, digestive system

In the movie *Kramer vs. Kramer*, Dustin Hoffman learns what Cancer energy is all about when his wife, Meryl Streep, leaves him and he suddenly finds himself as the sole caretaker of his young son. Adjectives like "nurturing," which were previously abstractions to Hoffman, now have become the reality.

The urge to nurture is Cancer's archetypal energy and the nurturing focuses on whatever is important to the individual—kids, home, career, spiritual life, health, animals, creativity. In some Cancer individuals, this nurturing energy is so powerful that they seek to comfort everything and everyone that crosses their paths.

As a water sign, Cancer is naturally intuitive and imaginative. Her intuition is so finely honed at times that she can walk into a room of people and instantly assess the mood of the crowd. Her imagination works the same way. Hand her anything—an image, an object, even an idea—and she weaves an elaborate tapestry around it. Her imagination is the wellspring of her creativity.

The nurturing energy of Cancer includes a deeply empathetic and compassionate nature. She instinctively feels what you feel, hurts when you hurt, and rejoices when you rejoice. Her empathy and compassion are part of what makes her an excellent healer. This healing ability may be expressed as a career in the medical profession, or it may be her avocation. It can encompass alternative healing techniques like homeopathy, the laying on of hands, or even psychic healing.

Most Cancers have a need for roots and a base of operation—preferably their own home. If it's near or on the water and includes a little land, so much the better. But she can set up a base of operation virtually anywhere. We have a Cancer friend whose camper is his "home," but he also house-sits for people, thus fulfilling the Cancerian energy for roots and home in that way.

Cancer's inner life is rich and varied, but she doesn't share it with just anyone. She must trust the people she lets into her most private world and until that trust is in place, she may seem elusive and enigmatic. It's difficult, in fact, for a Cancer to discuss what she feels because she doesn't really think about emotions; she simply *feels* them. She dislikes emotional confrontations, too, and will skitter off in the opposite direction, just like a crab, at the first hint of disagreement.

All three water signs can be psychic sponges, soaking up whatever energy is around them, so it's important for them to associate with positive, upbeat people. For Cancer, though, this is especially important. Her compassion and need to nurture can put her squarely in the center of someone else's energy, and when that energy is negative, it affects her. It may impact her mood, her health, or her frame of mind.

Vivian, a Cancer and an R.N. in a psychiatric unit, prepares herself for the daily onslaught of the ward by rising early to meditate, spending time with her animals, and fortifying her inner reserves against any negative energy. Even the message on her answering machine makes her intentions clear, "Please leave a positive message."

Astrologers say that the moon, our connection to our emotional and intuitive selves, never forgets. This capacity is certainly evident in Cancer, which the moon rules. Any memory that has strong emotions attached to it is permanently etched into Cancer's soul. She can relate, moment by moment, her first bicycle ride—not just the ride itself, but the quality of the air that day and the shade of the sky. In instances where her feelings were hurt or where she suffered a humiliation or deep trauma, her memory can cause her to cling to the hurt for years. Although she easily forgives a slight, she never forgets it. In extreme instances, emotional pain gets "stuck" in her body and may create health problems.

Cancer's shadow side can manifest as an emotional clinging—the crab hanging on for dear life to its shell—or acute emotional evasiveness. Cancer must learn when to let go and move on. In this respect, the energy of Capricorn, her polar opposite, can help. Capricorn is practical where Cancer sometimes gets stuck in nostalgia. During Capricorn's slow, steady climb through the world, he divests himself of emotional attachments that impede his progress. Once Cancer learns how to release, her life will unfold more smoothly.

Building a Personalized Workout

If you're reading this chapter because you're a Cancer, turn to the Capricorn postures in Chapter 11. Read through them, try them out, and consider incorporating them into your regular workout.

If you're reading this chapter as a result of your brainstorming activities, then read through the moon salutation. Your first attempt of these postures should be to acquaint yourself with the series and to develop an awareness of how your body feels. Are the postures easy or difficult for you? Do you feel tightness or discomfort? If so, where? How do you feel emotionally? If negative feelings occur as you're doing the postures, explore them. What's their source? What is the message? The second time you do the postures, use your *intent*.

Intent affirmation: *I now pull in the energy of Cancer—compassion, nurturing, tenderness.*

In creating your affirmation, use words that express what you're trying to accomplish. Maybe you need more empathy or deeper intuition right now. Or perhaps you need healing qualities. Whatever you need, include it in your affirmation.

A Gemini woman in one of Rob's classes had trouble doing the postures with intent. She said she couldn't do the postures, repeat the affirmation, *and* complete the visualization all at the same time. This seemed odd coming from a Gemini, who often juggles many tasks simultaneously. We suggested she say the affirmation before she began doing the postures with intent, and that she keep her visualization simple—just a single vivid image that depicted the outcome she sought.

When she tried this, she said she couldn't hold a single image in her mind because she was too focused on doing the postures. It was beginning to sound as if there were some other block at work here and we suggested that she simply do the postures and not worry about her intent. Then the truth came out. She was having trouble with her teenage son and when she did the moon salutation, all she could think about was how her son was the one who needed to change, not her. *He* needed to be more flexible, more considerate of other family members. In other words, her ego resisted the energy that her intuition said she needed.

When the situation or issue that you're working on becomes a point of resistance, it's best to just do the postures for their physical benefits, and to work on the issue separately. After several weeks, try them again with intent.

Intent visualization: As you're repeating your affirmation, imagine the end result of the situation or issue that you jotted in the brainstorming section. Let's say you would like to nurture a particular project, your own brainchild. Your visualization might be a mental image of yourself presenting your creative product to the powers that be, or perhaps an image of yourself celebrating the sale of the project.

The Moon Salutation

Like the moon rising after the sun sets, the moon and sun salutations complement one another. In both series, the postures flow one to another. You can either perform the moon salutation by holding the postures for a single breath, or you can slow down the movement and spend more time with each posture. The postures boost the entire body, stretch the arms, back, shoulders, and sides, and increase spinal flexibility.

Half-Moon

Stand at the center of your mat facing the side. Your back is straight, your shoulders relaxed. Raise your arms slowly out to the sides as you inhale. When they reach shoulder level, turn the palms up. Breathe in more air and continue raising your arms until your hands touch overhead. Now clasp your fingers together, except for your index fingers, and push through your fingertips in an elongated stretch (Figure 17-1A). Exhale, and stretch your upper body to the right as you continue reaching out through the fingertips in the **half-moon** (Figure 17-1B). You should be able to feel the stretch all along the left side of your body from the ankle, to the heel, to the fingers. The posture massages the liver and spleen and aids digestion. Hold at least one breath, then stretch up and down to the other side (Figure 17-1C).

The Goddess

Next, step out to your right, extend your arms straight out from the shoulders, and bring your shoulders back into the **star** position (Figure 17-2). Now turn your toes out to the sides, bend your forearms to a forty-five–degree angle and bend your knees. Sink down into the **goddess** (Figure 17-3A).

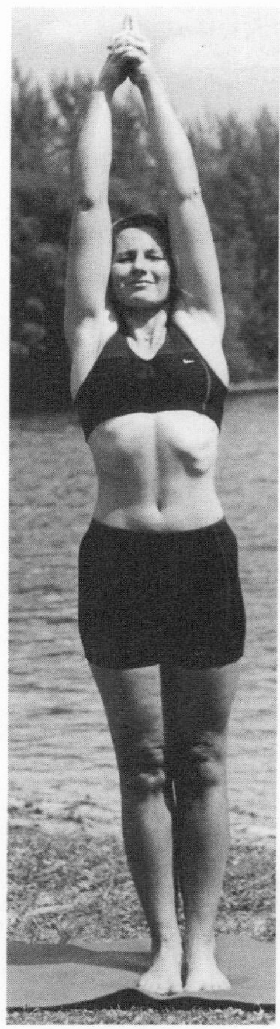

Figure 17-1A *Half-Moon* Position One

Figure 17-1B *Half-Moon* Position Two

Figure 17-1C *Half-Moon* Position Three

The goddess strengthens the calf and thigh muscles and stretches the shoulders and hips. It also builds your stamina. If you want to go deeper, bring your palms to your chest and sink down another couple of inches (Figure 17-3B).

Extended Side Angle Posture

Come back into the star posture. Then step farther out with your right foot and turn your toes on both feet to the right. Bend your right knee to ninety degrees and rest your forearm on your knee as you enter the modified version of the extended side angle posture. Now reach up with your left arm and look up to

Figure 17-2 The Star

Figure 17-3A The Goddess Position One

Figure 17-3B The Goddess Position Two

Figure 17-4A Extended Side Angle Posture Position One

your hand (Figure 17-4A). Next, extend your right hand to the mat and bring your left arm in line with your right to complete the **extended side angle** pose. (Figure 17-4B).

Extended-Leg Squat

From the extended side angle position, sink down into a squat and place your hands down in front of you. Turn the toes of your left foot upward. Begin with your arms straight (Figure 17-5). If you want to go farther in the **extended-leg squat**, bring your palms together at your chest.

Now you're halfway through the moon salutation. From here, squat to the other side, bending your left knee and straightening your right leg. Next, raise up into the extended side angle position, followed by the modified version of the pose with your forearm on your knee.

Figure 17-4B Extended Side Angle Posture Position Two

Figure 17-5 Extended-Leg Squat

Come up into the star position, then sink into the goddess. Go back into the star, step in so that both feet come together, and raise your arms up overhead clasping all but your index fingers. Bend to the right side in the half-moon, then to the other side. Reach straight overhead again, hold, then lower your hands into the prayer position with the palms together and the knuckles of the thumbs pressed into the solar plexus.

That completes the first round of the moon salutation. Now you can move into the intent phase by focusing on the keywords.

Variations

After the goddess and star, and before going into the modified variation of the extended side angle posture, you can bend your forward knee and sink into the warrior two position (Figure 5-2). Make sure your front foot is turned forward in the direction you are reaching.

Alternately, you can go into the **sideways leg stretch** in place of warrior two. Keep your legs straight, your hips facing the side wall, and your upper torso erect. Clasp your hands behind your back, push down, and arch your back (Figure 17-6A). Next, fold forward toward the front leg and simultaneously raise your arms above your head (Figure 17-6B).

Another variation can be added after the extended side angle posture. Keeping the legs in position, bring both hands inside the right foot, then sink down toward your forearms in the **forearm lunge** (Figure 17-7).

Figure 17-6A Sideways Leg Stretch Position One

You can also add several expanded leg stretches to the Cancer series, including them between your two extended leg squats. After your squats, move to center so your weight is equally balanced on each foot. Place your hands on the mat beneath your shoulders and bend forward, bringing the crown of your head toward the mat (Figure 17-8A).

Next, reach for your big toes. Raise your head up, arch your back, and fold down (Figure 17-8B). You can also walk your hands over to your right ankle and clasp both hands on the outside of the ankle. Fold down toward your leg. Hold for at least

Figure 17-6B Sideways Leg Stretch Position Two

Figure 17-7 Forearm Lunge

Figure 17-8A Expanded Leg Stretch Position One

Figure 17-8B Expanded Leg Stretch Position Two

Figure 17-8C Expanded Leg Stretch Position Three

one breath, then walk your hands to the other side and repeat (Figure 17-8C). You can then sink into the extended leg squat with the other leg and continue the series.

The Wave Breath

After you do the postures for the second time, lie on your back and do the wave breath. See Chapter 16 for more details.

18

Scorpio, the Scorpion

Theme:
Transformation
Keywords:
Passion, power, release, renewal
October 23–November 21
Fixed water
Ruled by Pluto
Rules sexual organs, rectum, reproductive system

No other energy in the zodiac possesses Scorpio's intensity. Just look at some of the areas it rules: nuclear power, fusion, the Mafia, death, taxes, reincarnation, sex, metaphysics, and transformation at the deepest levels. When this energy is used with intent, it can be incredibly powerful. With this in mind, remember the adage: be careful what you ask for because you just might get it.

Of the three water signs, Scorpio's energy is the most strong-willed, intense, and passionate. Where Pisces vacillates and Cancer avoids, Scorpio is direct, sometimes confrontational, and always relentless when passion is ignited.

Like Aries, Scorpios aren't afraid of very much. As a fixed sign, they have far more endurance than Aries. Long after Aries has gotten bored and moved on, Scorpio is still in there digging for facts, plowing ahead, overcoming every obstacle in the way.

Scorpio individuals are suspicious of easy answers and this suspicion impels them to delve deeply into whatever interests them. If there's a secret to be found, they find it. If that archaeological dig possibly holds the secret of the ancient world, they'll uncover it. If there's life beyond our galaxy, Scorpio travels the universe to find it. They are experts at perceiving the reality behind the facade, and they probe until they find what they intuitively know is there.

Before the discovery of Pluto, Mars ruled Scorpio. But Mars is fiery and aggressive, the antithesis of Scorpio. Pluto fits the bill so much better. It orbits at the very edge of our solar system, four billion miles from our sun, so distant that it's barely more than a glimmer of light in the lens of a powerful telescope, and that's on a clear night. It's wrapped in enigma, almost as mysterious today as when it was discovered in 1930. In astrology, Pluto symbolizes power—the power we seek, the power we hold over others, the power they hold over us. Just when we get too comfortable, too set in our ways, its energy sweeps through our lives, rips down the structures we've built, and tears apart the foundations we've laid. And, in the rubble, something new is born. Pluto is the phoenix of Greek mythology, the ultimate transformer—and so is Scorpio.

Thanks to the raw intuitive powers of the sign, Scorpios often have some talent at which they excel. Music, art, drama, writing, photography—whatever it is, they bring their piercing perceptions to it. The talent may or may not become their work, but it's always a source of pleasure for themselves and for others. This talent can also be Scorpio's salvation, the salve that soothes his soul.

Scorpio individuals come in two broad types: those who don't understand who they are and those who do. This might be said of any sign, but with Scorpio, it's the absolute bottom line. The first type embodies the shadow of the sign. They want power purely for the sake of power, and once they have it, they wield it just to make sure the rest of us know they have it. Their hunger for power can show up in any number of ways, but sex is often one form of expression. Another favorite of this type: money as power. This sign is the archetypal controller.

One thing is for sure with this type: pull in some of the energy of the opposite sign, Taurus, and much of the shadow is toned down. Most of the time, Taurus couldn't care less about power. Where Scorpio has to plunder the underworld for answers, Taurus walks out into her garden and finds the same answers. Where Scorpio gets even, Taurus just writes you out of her life for good. For Scorpio, sex is serious business. It may be serious business for Taurus, too, but first it's fun and sensual.

The other type of Scorpio is the one who lives with a higher awareness of what he's here to do. He is driven, yes, but he knows what drives him. He probes, but understands why. This is the type of Scorpio who leaves his imprint on the people who love him and on the larger world that may never know him. In some way, he transforms our collective perception of what is possible.

On a daily basis, all this energy often translates into a taciturn individual. His piercing perceptions make him an excellent teacher, spy, detective, actor, funeral director, or trust attorney. Whatever his work, he brings his quest for deeper meaning into it. He simply cannot separate the quest from the rest of his life.

Building a Personalized Workout

If you're reading this chapter because you're a Scorpio, then turn to Chapter 9 and read through the postures for Taurus. Consider including these postures in your regular workout, especially if you're going through a difficult or intense period in your life. If nothing else, the Taurus postures will ground you and get you to lighten up.

If you're reading this chapter because the brainstorming activities indicate that you need Scorpio energy, read through the following postures. Try them first just to see how they feel to you. Be aware of your body; be fully there, rather than thinking about all of the stuff you have to do, so that you notice how your body and mind react to the postures. Once you've completed your first round, do them again with *intent.*

Intent affirmation: *I'm now drawing in power, piercing perception, and psychic ability into my life.*

If these particular words don't fit your goals, substitute your own descriptive phrases for Scorpio's energy. Create an affirmation that's simple and concise, but specific to your needs. As you're doing the postures, repeat the affirmation silently.

You can also use your affirmation before falling asleep at night or as you're waking up in the morning. At these times, your unconscious mind is receptive to such messages. The more often you say the affirmation, backing it with sincerity and emotional conviction, the quicker your unconscious believes it.

Intent visualization: Keep it simple, but vivid. If your goal is to pull more power into your life, then focus on a mental image in which those qualities are evident in a particular situation. Perhaps you have a domineering boss who treats you like an indentured servant. A possible visualization might be of you standing up to your boss over a project in which you believe. Imagine what you're wearing, how you stand, your voice, your confidence, and your *power.* Feel the power you emanate. Imagine the place where this situation occurs—the color of the walls, the size of the windows, the furniture. Imagine your boss smiling, nodding, accepting your argument about the project, or congratulating you on a job well done.

Don't worry about how you're going to arrive at this final scene; simply focus on the end result and trust the process. If you have trouble creating a visualization, then look for a sketch, photograph, or even a physical object that is comparable to what you want. Fix it in your mind's eye and use it to visualize your end result. While you're doing the intent part of the Scorpio postures, repeat your affirmation several times and hold the visualization in your mind. Then release it.

The Camel/Abdominal Stretch Series

Power and renewal. Opening up. Flowing with the energy. The camel/abdominal stretch series absorbs the energy of Scorpio through back-bending positions that stretch and tone the abdominal muscles, and counter poses that allow you to contract those same muscles and massage your internal organs. These postures also improve flexibility of the spine and neck.

Seated Kneeling Pose

We begin with several kneeling postures. Start by sitting between your knees in the **seated kneeling** pose. If you can't sit all the way down, then stay up on your knees. Relax a few moments. Close your eyes and quiet your mind. Focus on your breath, letting go of your thoughts. Alternately, if you are entering the intent phase of the workout, focus on the keywords for Scorpio: *power, transforming, renewing, releasing.*

Seated Kneeling Stretch

Stretch your arms up overhead as you inhale, then fold forward reaching out as far as you can. Relax your shoulders and sink further down. Feel the sensation of water flowing over you in the **seated kneeling stretch** (Figures 18-1A and 18-1B). Stretch up and forward at least two more times.

Chin Lock

Now come into a kneeling position. Clasp your hands on the back of your thighs. Drop your head, round your shoulders, and exhale all of the air from your lungs. Pull in your belly in an exaggerated manner and hold the **chin lock** pose for up to ten seconds. You are stretching your neck, tensing your abdominal muscles, and gently moving your internal organs (Figure 18-2).

Kneeling Abdominal Stretch

Inhale, raise your head and your chin. Still clasping your thighs, push your hips forward and bring your shoulder blades and elbows closer together. Arch your back and stretch your abdominal muscles. Again hold the **kneeling abdominal stretch** for up to ten seconds (Figure 18-3).

Now you are stretching the abdominal muscles as well as the thigh and shoulder muscles. Exhale down into the chin lock again. Inhale into the abdominal stretch. Repeat the combination at least one more time.

The Camel

Come back into the extended abdominal stretch again and hold. This time, inhale and exhale through the nose, expanding the diaphragm as you inhale and contracting it as you exhale. You can stay here and hold for at least five or six breaths, or you can go into the **camel**. If you're not familiar with the posture, try the modified version first. Come up onto your toes and reach back for your heels. Push your hips forward and drop your head back.

Alternately, you can go into the full expression of the pose by keeping your ankles flat and reaching for your heels. Again, push your hips forward and drop your head back. Feel the stretch across the abdominal muscles and thighs, as well as the chest and neck (Figure 18-4). Hold for five or six more deep breaths.

Figure 18-1A Seated Kneeling Stretch Position One

Figure 18-1B Seated Kneeling Stretch Position Two

Figure 18-2 Chin Lock

Figure 18-3 Kneeling Abdominal Stretch

Figure 18-4 The Camel

Figure 18-5 Child's Pose

Child's Pose

Sit back onto your heels again and fold forward into the **child's pose.** Bring your arms alongside your legs and relax your shoulders. In this pose, you are not only relaxing the spinal ligaments and stretching the back muscles, but also gently contracting your abdominal muscles and relieving the compression on the lumbar discs—pads of cartilage located between the vertebrae. Sink your buttocks toward your heels (Figure 18-5).

Figure 18-6A Kneeling Chest Opener Position One

Figure 18-6B Kneeling Chest Opener Position Two

Kneeling Chest Opener

From the child's pose, clasp your hands behind you. Straighten your arms and lift your arms as high as you can, stretching the shoulders and opening the chest (Figure 18-6A). The **kneeling chest opener** stretches the chest and strengthens the shoulders. It also serves as a counter pose to the abdominal stretches, since you are contracting your abdominal muscles. Hold for five or six breaths. Now roll onto the crown of your head and raise your arms higher (Figure 18-6B). Hold for another five or six breaths.

The Dolphin

Next, from the child's pose come onto your hands and knees in the table pose. Inhale and exhale in the tilted dog and cat stretch (Figures 9-1 and 9-2). Straighten your legs and come down onto your forearms for the **dolphin**. Push back through your tailbone and drop the crown of the head toward the mat (Figure 18-7). Raise your head, pushing your chin forward, and bring your head forward between your hands. If that's too challenging, you can practice the dolphin from your knees and forearms. From either position, go back and forth five or six times.

Figure 18-7 The Dolphin

The Scorpion

From the dolphin pose, either on your knees or with your legs straight, raise one leg and drop the crown of your head toward the mat as you go into the **modified scorpion** (Figure 18-8). An inverted pose, the scorpion stimulates the thyroid and pituitary glands, which control sexual energies. Hold for three or four breaths, then switch legs.

Clearly the most challenging posture in the series, the **full scorpion** pose is best practiced near a wall if you aren't familiar with it. Come into the dolphin again with your legs straight and your hands placed about two feet from the wall. Raise your chin and move your head forward toward your hands. Lift one leg and kick up with the other, bringing both legs overhead and against the wall. Push down with your forearms and arch your back, raising your head slightly higher (Figure 18-9). Hold for five or six breaths.

As you become more proficient at the scorpion, move your feet away from the wall after you enter the pose, bringing your legs directly above your head. When you gain confidence with the scorpion, you can begin entering the pose without relying on a wall for support.

Figure 18-8 Modified Scorpion

Figure 18-9 Full Scorpion

The Firm Pose

Sit between your heels and place your hands with your fingers forward on the mat beside your hips. Now drop your head back, stretching your abdominal muscles and the front of your thighs. Hold for three or four breaths. The modified **firm pose** increases suppleness of the legs and helps cure pains in the joints of the legs. It also serves as a counter pose to the dolphin and scorpion.

Variations

For a more challenging variation of the firm pose, come down onto your forearms (Figure 18-10A). Hold for five or six breaths. If you can keep your knees down, lower yourself onto your back and bring your arms overhead, clasping onto your elbows (Figure 18-10B). Hold for another five or six breaths. These deeper postures stretch the abdominal muscles and increase the flexibility of the lower spine.

Figure 18-10A Firm Pose Position One

Figure 18-10B Firm Pose Position Two

For another variation, extend one leg forward from the modified firm pose, then lean back onto your forearms or all the way down onto your back (Figure 18-11). Again, you are stretching the abdominal muscles and also increasing flexibility in the knee joints. Hold for several breaths, then come up and fold down toward your extended leg as you contract the abdominal muscles (Figure 18-12). Anyone with knee problems should use caution in this pose. Hold the **heel-to-hip forward bend** for several breaths, then raise up, switch legs, and repeat.

The Wave Breath

After completing the intent round of the series, unwind from the firm pose and lie on your back in preparation for the breathing exercise related to the water signs. See Chapter 16 for an explanation of the wave breath.

Figure 18-11 Extended Leg Firm Pose

Figure 18-12 Heel-to-Hip Forward Bend

19

PISCES, THE FISH

Theme:
Deep healing
Keywords:
Compassion, inspiration, the quest
February 19–March 20
Mutable water
Ruled by Neptune
Rules the feet and lymphatic system

In the movie *The Sixth Sense*, a little boy is literally haunted by the ghosts he sees. He doesn't just see them sometimes—he sees them all the time. They speak to him, they touch him, they tell him things. He has no one to talk to about these experiences until he meets a psychologist played by Bruce Willis. The shocker comes when we discover that Willis is a ghost who does not realize he's dead.

From the stunning opening to the dramatic conclusion, this movie embodies Piscean energy. It's the most mystical and compassionate of the twelve signs, the true bleeding heart of the zodiac.

The symbol for the sign—two fish swimming in opposite directions—characterizes the essential dichotomy in the Piscean nature. The typical Pisces is always in a quandary about what to do. Should he go right or left? To Tokyo or Topeka?

Given his choice, he would sit in a hammock in the warm sun and daydream or read. To him, the real world lies within, in the labyrinthine beauty of his own imagination. He shuts his eyes and that inner world lights up like a stage. His dreams are its tapestries. The voices he hears in this private world are more real than the voices of his spouse, his children, his boss. He is Walter Mitty.

That role is fine with him. The problem is that the external world presses against him, making demands, expecting him to be this way or that, neither of which fits who he is. Let the fish dream, please. When he's in his dreamy mood, he accesses places in the universe the rest of us will never touch because we simply aren't wired the way he is.

Edgar Cayce, who was probably the most documented psychic of the twentieth century, was a Pisces and a good example of this kind of "wiring." He gave thousands of past life and health readings during his lifetime, all while he was asleep. This ability to access very deep places in the human psyche is also the fount of creativity. Listen to Chopin or George Harrison, both of them Pisces, for the depth of that fount. Watch Liz Taylor in *Cat on a Hot Tin Roof.* Listen to Liza Minnelli belt out songs.

The creative piece of the Piscean archetype is the ability to make the rest of the world vanish when he's doing what he loves. The world vanishes so completely, in fact, that only the exquisite distillation of the emotion remains, as perfect as a pearl.

The Piscean compassion is born of that same creative fount. That's why Pisces people are often found working in hospitals, hospices, nursing homes, and psychiatric units. They don't just feel what their patients feel; they become that pain, that despair, that agony. It seizes them, haunts them until they just can't stand it anymore. And that's when they extend their hands, touching the pain and the despair to make it go away, to *heal* it.

In the opening scenes of the movie *Resurrection*, Ellen Burstyn and her husband are zipping up a highway in his new car. He loses control, the car plunges over the side of a cliff, and Burstyn wakes up in a hospital. Her husband is dead, and the doctor informs her she will never again walk.

Over the subsequent months, Burstyn heals herself and ultimately becomes a healer of incomparable power. In one particularly moving scene, she lies beside a deformed patient and puts her arms around the woman and literally takes on the woman's deformity. She then transmutes it, working it through and out of her own body. Alchemy—the absolute best of the Piscean energy.

On the shadow side, though, the news isn't good. It's called escape, and it's sought through any means necessary: booze, drugs, cults, sex, work, sacrifice. This darker element of Pisces is evident in the quietly suffering type who takes care of an ailing parent for thirty years. It's seen in the quiet terror of an abused wife. Saint, victim, alcoholic: it's part and parcel of the Piscean shadow.

So toss in a little energy from Virgo, the Pisces polarity, to clean things up and shed some light on the picture. Virgo's quest for the ideal certainly doesn't include the suffering victim or the stumbling drunk. The analytical abilities of Virgo can provide tremendous strength to Pisces and vanquish the shadow, but only if the fish comes out of the dreamy waters of his own mind long enough to draw on it.

Building a Personalized Workout

The Pisces/Virgo polarity is one of the most difficult to master because the two signs are so diametrically opposed. This is an instance, however, where Astro-Yoga can work as a bridge, especially when the postures are used in conjunction with an affirmation and visualization.

If you're reading this chapter because you're a Pisces, then turn to Chapter 10 and read through the Virgo postures. It's important to include them in your regular workout. If you're reading this chapter because the brainstorming activity indicates you need Piscean energy, you should try the postures the first time just to acquaint yourself with them. As you do so, take a reading on how your body reacts to the postures and how you feel about them. Be fully aware of your body as you go through the series.

Your second time through the postures should be done with *intent*. This involves two steps: an affirmation and a visualization.

Intent affirmation: *I now draw compassion, sensitivity, and inspiration into my life.*

You can alter the affirmation to fit the particular situation you are addressing. However, keep the affirmation concise, simple, and tailored to your present needs. The affirmation should be repeated several times before moving into the intent mode of the workout.

Intent visualization: What's your ultimate goal? Define it and create an image that embodies the end result of what you're trying to pull into your life. Perhaps you're working on a project and have run into a block of some kind. Your visualization might then be of a finished product. If you have trouble imagining that product, create some aspect of it that seems feasible. It helps to create a visualization if you have something tangible to work with.

Upward Boat/Incline Plane Series

In the upward boat position, the image of the body floating on water easily comes to mind. You are floating in the energy of Pisces. In the fish posture, you drift into the depths. The feet are the focal body part of Pisces, and so the cobbler is an appropriate pose since you bow toward your feet. As you rise into the incline plane, the counter position of the upward boat, the feet come into play as you work them into the mat. The upward boat postures strengthen and tone the abdominal and lower back muscles and open the chest, while the incline plane strengthens the back, leg, and shoulder muscles.

When you move into the intent phase of the Pisces workout, you might see yourself floating on water as you enter the poses. Focus on deep healing, the theme of the series. As you do the postures, repeat your affirmation several times or simply say the keywords for Pisces: *compassion, inspiration, sensitivity.* Where in your life can you make use of this energy?

Upward Boat

You begin the series relaxing on your back in the corpse position. When you are ready, bend your knees, clasp your hands below your thighs, and rock forward and back several times. Rock up into a seated position and place your hands behind your hips with the fingers forward. Keep your shoulders back, your chest forward, and your elbows bent. Lean back and raise your bent knees off the mat (Figure 19-1A). Hold for three or four breaths.

Figure 19-1A Upward Boat Position One

See if you are able to straighten your legs and come into the second position (Figure 19-1B). The next option calls for you to straighten your arms parallel with your legs (Figure 19-1C). Raise your chest and arch your back. If your torso hunches forward when you straighten your legs, you need to practice the first posture until your abdominal muscles are stron- ger. Hold the **upward boat** for five or six breaths.

Figure 19-1B Upward Boat Position Two

Figure 19-1C Upward Boat Position Three

Figure 19-2 Incline Plane

Incline Plane

For **incline plane**, lower your legs to the mat and place your hands behind your hips, fingers forward. Now raise your hips and plant your feet firmly down. See if you can form a straight line along your neck, back, and legs (Figure 19-2). Hold for three or four breaths.

Lower your body, then go immediately into the upward boat again, starting with position one and continuing on to whichever position you want to practice. Hold for five or six breaths. Raise up into the incline plane again and hold for three or four breaths. Repeat the boat/incline plane combination one more time.

If you need to take a break, relax in the corpse position when you complete your last set.

Side Incline

When you're ready to continue, come into a seated position with legs extended. You might start with the modified side incline. Roll your hips to the right and come up onto your right knee, planting your right hand in alignment with the right knee and extended left leg. Your right foot either can be in line with the body or at a ninety-degree angle. Now stretch your left arm up, push your hips forward, and look up toward your raised hand. Drop your upper shoulder back (Figure 19-3A). Next, extend your arm above your ear and stretch through your fingertips and left heel (Figure 19-3B.)

Figure 19-3A Modified Side Incline Position One

Figure 19-3B Modified Side Incline Position Two

This posture stretches the sides of your body and strengthens your shoulders, lower back, hips, and legs. It also increases flexibility of your spine and improves your endurance.

From the modified posture, you can go directly into the **side incline** by straightening both legs, the left on top of the right. Your body remains open to the right, with your right hand planted on the mat and your left arm raised, forming a straight line with the right arm (Figure 19-3C). If your midsection tends to slump down, stay with the modified version until you've gained more strength in your lower back.

Try raising your hips up a little higher. If you want to go further, extend your arm above your ear so that you form a straight line between your left heel and left hand (Figure 19-3D). Take a few breaths, then raise your arm toward the ceiling again and drop your shoulder back, opening your chest (Figure 19-3E).

After completing the side incline postures on one side, sit up again, roll to the other side, and repeat the postures.

Figure 19-3C ***Side Incline Position One***

Figure 19-3D Side Incline Position Two

Figure 19-3E Side Incline Position Three

Butterfly-Cobbler

Figure 19-4 Butterfly-Cobbler Pose

Come into a seated position and bring the soles of your feet together. Clasp your toes with both hands and pull the heels toward your groin. Sit up straight and butterfly your knees up and down several times. Then lower your elbows to your calves and press down, opening your hips. When you're ready, slide your feet forward twelve to eighteen inches. Still holding onto your toes, fold your upper body forward and bring your forehead toward your toes. The **butterfly-cobbler** pose opens your hips and lengthens your spine. Hold for five or six breaths (Figure 19-4).

Extended Upward Boat

From the butterfly-cobbler, clasp your first two fingers around your big toes. Sit up and lift your feet, straightening your legs and spreading them apart in the **extended upward boat**. Hold for three or four breaths. If you want to go further, bring your heels together (Figure 19-5). Hold for three or four more breaths.

Figure 19-5 Extended Upward Boat

Figure 19-6A The Fish

The Fish

Lie on your back again. This time slide your hands, palms down, beneath your buttocks. Bring your elbows closer together, arch your back, and place the crown of your head on the mat. Take several deep breaths in the **fish** pose, pushing your belly up as you inhale and letting it sink down as you exhale (Figure 19-6A).

After the fish, you can move from form to intent. Keep in mind that you don't need to rigorously follow every posture. Some days you may want to shorten your workout or, as you become more familiar with the postures, you may do a couple of the postures in form and others only during the intent phase. Other days you may want to intensify your workout and add some of the variations below.

Variations

You can begin the series by rocking back and forth and coming into balance, keeping your feet off the mat. Continue clasping your hands to your thighs and lean farther back, while raising your chest higher. From there you can straighten your legs or go into position three of the upward boat.

From the side incline, raise your upper leg while reaching up. Hold for a few breaths. Next, clasp your big toe with your first two fingers, making sure to maintain your stability and spinal alignment, including your neck. If possible, straighten your leg.

Figure 19-6B Fish Variation

Figure 19-6C Fish Variation

From the fish position, you can lift both legs and reach out with your arms so they are parallel with your legs. Bring your palms together (Figure 19-6B). Hold for five or six breaths. Finally, if your hips are flexible, try the fish in the full lotus position with the palms pressed together at the chest (Figure 19-6C).

The Wave Breath

After the intent series of postures, relax on your back in preparation for the wave breath. See Chapter 16 for a full explanation.

20

Relaxation and Meditation

At the end of your workout take at least five minutes, preferably more, to relax and hopefully enter a light meditative state. The relaxation not only provides a means to cool down, but it also allows you to assimilate the energy that you garnered through your session. If you skip the relaxation, you miss an important and rewarding part of your workout. It's like working hard all week at your job, and then deciding not to bother getting your check. You may have been happy and successful in your work, but you didn't get compensated. With yoga, the relaxation is your payoff.

Lie on your back in the corpse pose or *savasana*. Your legs are apart, your arms are at your sides with your palms turned up. Check your body—make sure that your neck, shoulders, back, chest, hips, and legs are comfortable. Close your eyes.

Begin with at least a couple of minutes of deep diaphragmatic breathing. Inhale through your nose and push your belly up. Let your belly slowly sink down as you exhale through your nose, and feel yourself becoming more and more relaxed with each exhalation.

Shift to gentle nostril breathing. If you were working on a specific situation in your life during your workout, say the affirmation that you used. Stay focused and specific. If you created a visualization, re-create the image and feelings associated with it. When your mind starts wandering, return to the affirmation or the image that you created.

If you're not working with any particular situation, you might coordinate your breathing with the following affirmation: *Inhale relaxation; exhale tension. Inhale health; exhale illness. Inhale prosperity; exhale poverty. Inhale peace; exhale conflict. Inhale relaxation; exhale tension.*

After the affirmation and visualization, you can continue with your relaxation by turning your focus to your body and first tensing, then relaxing, your arms and shoulders, legs and feet, back and chest. Begin by tensing your fists, arms, and shoulders. Lift your arms an inch or two off the mat. Now curl your toes, tense your feet, calves, knees, thighs, and hips. Lift your legs slightly off the mat along with your arms. Now tense your chest and back, your belly and buttocks. Squeeze all the muscles in your face as you inhale and hold your breath. When you can't hold any longer, exhale with a sigh and relax all of your muscles. Notice the difference between your tensed and relaxed muscles.

Now, as you relax, imagine a wave of relaxation washing down your body from the crown of your head. Imagine invisible fingers massaging your scalp. Now the invisible fingers move over your forehead and your temples. Feel the massaging sensation working gently around your eye sockets and along your cheekbones. The relaxing feeling moves down your jaw toward your chin. Leave a little gap between your teeth and let your tongue come down from the roof of your mouth.

The wave of relaxation moves down your neck, over your shoulders, and along your arms from your upper arms to your elbows, forearms, wrists, and hands. Relax your fingers and let the palms of your hands relax.

Now the relaxation moves over your chest, back, and sides. Let your lower back relax. Feel the hipbones relax in the hip sockets. Your belly relaxes. Feel your buttocks and the backs of the thighs melting away. The tops of your thighs relax. Feel your kneecaps floating on your knees. The backs of the knees relax. The shins relax and all the muscles in the calves relax. Ankles, feet, and toes relax. Feel the bottoms of your feet relax. Next, let your internal organs relax down toward your spine.

Allow your mind to relax. Slow down the internal chatter. Become aware of what you're thinking and feeling. Gently release your thoughts. Find a space between two thoughts. Hold it. Sink deeper.

By now you may have entered a light meditative state. But if you are bombarded by thoughts and have difficulty separating yourself from your thoughts, focus on your breath. Imagine your breath like a stream of white light entering through your nostrils, flowing into the lungs, and out again. You might also imagine the flame of a candle burning on your brow between your eyes. With your eyelids closed, turn your gaze upward and slightly inward as you focus on the imaginary flame. As you sink into a meditative state, you can release the imaginary flame. But if you are distracted by your thoughts, return to the flame. This process is known as passive meditation and can be both relaxing and a means to assimilating the energy you gained from your workout.

Healing Energy Meditation

If you're not working with a particular situation or objective, or you feel that you've done all you can do, you can also visualize healing energy flowing through your body. Imagine a silver light moving into the bottom of your left foot and up through your leg all the way to your hip. Then see the light moving through your abdomen across your chest toward your right shoulder. The energy moves down your arm and out your hand. Then the cycle is repeated as the light flows into the bottom of your right foot. See the energy traveling through the circuit that you've created as it goes around and around. You can use this image for healing physical injuries or for relieving stress and bringing more energy into your life. Hold the image for about five minutes.

Star Meditation

Another active meditation, known as the star meditation or the Tibetan Star Meditation, was introduced to us by John Perkins, author of *The World Is As You Dream*. The meditation provides an excellent means to destroy the barriers keeping you from completing a task or goal, following a dream, or finding yourself a dream. It blends well with Astro-Yoga.

Begin by returning to the visualization that you used at the start of the relaxation. Focus on the image and create the emotional sensations that would accompany your success in achieving the goal or dream you hope to achieve. Now let go of your thoughts, releasing the image, and focus on the field of darkness in front of you. Gradually, see a point of light forming. Slowly, it begins to grow and intensify. Watch it expand into a brilliant silver star that fills the entire field of your vision.

Now move the bright star to the crown of your head, or the crown chakra. See and feel its energy growing more and more intense as it continues to expand. Then, suddenly, when it can't intensify any further, the star explodes and destroys the barriers blocking you from achieving your goal.

Now see the star forming again at the crown chakra. The energy intensifies as the star expands and expands, then bursts with a release of incredible energy. The blockages are blown away again. Repeat the process one more time.

Next, move the silver star to your heart chakra. See and feel the energy intensifying as the star glows and grows. It continues to grow larger and hotter until the energy explodes, smashing the barriers obstructing your way. Again, see the star re-forming at your heart. It becomes brighter and brighter, glowing with a new intensity. As it expands and expands once again, see and feel the star exploding and wiping away all that blocks you from achieving your dream. Repeat the process one more time.

Now move the silver star to a point between your navel and groin, the second chakra. Known as *svadhisthana*, the second chakra is the center of physical, sexual, and creative energy. Feel the star's heat intensifying. See it becoming brighter and brighter as it expands and expands even further. See it explode sending forth its energy and annihilating all the barriers to achieving your goal. Watch again as the silver star swells and brightens until you can see nothing but its brightness, and then feel it erupt and blast apart, removing all obstacles from your path. Repeat the sequence one more time.

Finally, see the star re-forming directly in front of you. Watch as it gradually shrinks away to a point, then vanishes altogether. Open your eyes and sit quietly a few moments knowing that the power you have released will obliterate the blocks that are holding you back from finding your dream or following it.

Following a Dream

Remember that if you are pursuing a dream or searching for a dream, make it realistic. Don't select a dream that is merely a fantasy. These dreams seem intriguing, but are ones that you wouldn't actually want to create.

After you've found your dream or decided to search for one, apply your intent during the yoga postures through the energy of the signs. Visualize the final results of your goal or dream. See what it would look like and how you would feel about it. Create this visualization on a daily basis as well as whenever you relax and go into the star meditation. Take action to make the dream come true. Do something every day toward that goal, even if you only allow yourself ten or fifteen minutes of the day. For example, if you want to write a book, write at least one page a day.

Continue the process three or four times a week, through the Astro-Yoga postures, by meditating, visualizing, and acting, and watch the results. Some days, you may want to limit your time to just a couple of minutes. Other days, you might want to take much longer. Some big dreams, such as reversing the degradation of the environment, may take a while to manifest. But others, such as removing writer's block or finding a solution to a problem, can be resolved in no time at all.

When we were searching for a new house, we eventually found one that met all of our needs. But the price was too high and the owner seemed unwilling to negotiate. We focused on the house in our workouts for two or three days, particularly working with the moon salutation, which brings in Cancer energy. During the relaxation, we visualized ourselves happily living in the house, and we blasted away at the barriers through the star meditation. But we realized that we were becoming too attached. So we released the house at the end of the relaxation session following a workout. We liked the house, but if it didn't work out, there would be another for us.

The next day, our realtor told us that the owner was willing to lower the price if we would accept the house "as is" without any required repairs after the inspection. Since we knew the house was in good condition, we agreed. As it turned out, the owner fixed the most serious problem, one that would have cost us several hundred dollars.

Giving Thanks

At the end of your relaxation or meditation, feel yourself gradually coming alert. You might slowly count to five. On three, turn your head from side to side, bring your knees toward your chest, place your hands below your knees, and gently rock from side to side. Then come over onto your right side, release your hand, and relax. On four, come into a seated position. Keep your eyes closed. Stay focused on your breath for another minute or two. Breathing gently, imagine your breath like a stream of white light coming into your nostrils and out again.

On five, open your eyes. Notice how relaxed and refreshed you feel. Give thanks for having the opportunity and ability to practice yoga.

Appendix A

What the Signs Rule

The list below shows the general areas that each sign rules. If, for instance, you had a house question, you would want to pull in the energy of Cancer. The question-and-answer section addresses specific situations.

Aries: self, physical characteristics, overall health, launching anything new, leadership, our social masks

Taurus: money management, personal values, gardening, working with the hands, possessions

Gemini: taking tests, schooling, workshops, short trips, siblings, relatives, neighbors, routine activities, communication of any kind, the conscious mental process

Cancer: home, family, ancestral roots, parent who is primary nurturer, sense of belonging, unconscious memories, connection to the collective unconscious, intuition

Leo: pleasure, creativity, children, love affairs, meditation, gambling, pets

Virgo: general health, work, work conditions, services performed for others, hygiene, communication (the details)

Libra: marriage, one-on-one partnerships, cooperation, the arts

Scorpio: taxes, profound spiritual concerns, insurance, partner's earning capacity, alimony, joint finances, death, funerals, funeral homes, sexuality, issues and situations that we don't like to deal with consciously

Sagittarius: higher education, the higher mind, long-distance travel, publishing, philosophy, religious and spiritual beliefs, foreign cultures, justice, the legal system, attorneys

Capricorn: career and profession, the authoritarian parent, ambition, our role in the larger world

Aquarius: networking, people we hang out with, groups we belong to, goals, inventions, astrology, humanitarian concerns, individuality, computers and computer networking, the Internet and the Web, group projects

Pisces: hospitals, prisons, corporations, institutions of any kind, anything behind the scenes, power we disown, mystical experiences, dreams, fantasies, our connection to the divine

Questions and Answers

I'm looking for a new house. What energy should I tap to facilitate my search?
Cancer and the moon salutation postures.

I need to whittle down my debt and bring in more income. What energy and postures are good for that?
Taurus energy and the cobra/downward-facing dog series of postures are best for managing money. To increase your income, Scorpio and the camel/abdominal stretch postures are best. Scorpio rules other people's resources, which you definitely want to tap.

I have chronic health problems. What energy and postures are appropriate for an overall improvement in health?
The theme of Pisces is deep healing. This series serves to reach into the deeper causes of illness. However, any yoga postures, done consistently and with intent, will improve your general health. For specific health problems, note the parts of the body ruled by the various signs and do those postures.

My career seems to have stalled. What can I do to get it moving again?
Capricorn is the energy you want to tap for general career concerns.

I'm planning a trip abroad. What energy do I need to facilitate my trip and make sure things go smoothly?
Sagittarius and the side prayer/triangle series are the obvious choices here because Sagittarius rules long-distance travel. Gemini, the polarity of Sagittarius, and the forehead-to-knee postures should also be included.

My relationship with my children isn't going well. What can I do to smooth things out?
Cancer, as ruler of the home and family, and the moon salutation postures are helpful in terms of nurturing. Leo and the sun salutation postures are excellent for general dealings with children.

My brother and I don't see eye to eye on anything. What can I do to improve our relationship?
Gemini rules siblings and communication, so the forehead-to-knee series would be a good place to start. For the bigger picture, include postures for Gemini's polarity, Sagittarius.

I'm looking for a new job. What can I do to facilitate and speed up my search for the ideal job?
To some extent, the energy you need depends on the kind of job you're looking for. A job in the computer industry, for instance, would be related to Aquarius. The communication area would belong to Gemini. Public relations would be Libra's

domain. Hospital work would be related to Pisces. Refer to the chapters on specific signs.

In general, the postures for Virgo, which rules the area of health and work, would be beneficial. Leo postures would bolster your self-confidence.

I want to get married, but my significant other isn't too keen on the idea. What energy can I pull in to change this situation?

Libra rules all partnerships, including marriage, so the balance postures would be beneficial. The Taurus postures would be beneficial as well because of the romanticism and stability associated with the sign.

I'm going to be taking exams soon. What energy should I pull in to help me do well on the tests?

Gemini's forehead-to-knee postures are excellent for any kind of studying or tests. You can also do postures related to the kinds of tests you're going to take. College entrance exams would call for the Sagittarian postures. Real estate exams would call for Cancer postures. Acting auditions are Leo's domain.

My spouse and I are going through a divorce. What energy can I tap to assure an equitable settlement?

This is clearly Scorpio's territory because you're dealing with joint finances. Sagittarian postures might also be called for because you're dealing with a legal matter.

I have a creative project I'm trying to sell. What energy should I try to pull in?

The sun salutation for Leo governs creativity in general. You can also do postures related to the project itself. A book or movie script would call for the energy of Sagittarius. A painting would call for Taurus or Libra. If the creative project is part of your career, as opposed to a hobby, then Capricorn postures would be beneficial.

If you are blocked with a creative project and need new ideas or to get the energy flowing again, Aquarius and Gemini postures would serve your purpose.

I'm facing surgery soon. What can I do to make sure it goes well?
The postures for Pisces would work for this situation. You can also do the postures related to certain body parts. Surgery on lungs, shoulders, and hands would fall under Gemini's domain. Surgery on bones would fall under Capricorn. Refer to the specific signs to see which body parts they rule.

I need to revamp my public image. Where should I start?
Start with the warrior postures for Aries, then do postures related to the image you want to create. If you want to appear more magnetic, go for the Leo postures. If you want to seem more balanced and artistic, Libra is the natural choice.

Appendix B

Sanskrit Names for Postures

Yoga postures typically come with two names: one in Sanskrit, which is usually long and often ending with *asana*, and the other in English. The use of the two names links yoga, as practiced in the West, with its Eastern heritage. For simplicity's sake, we've used the English terms almost exclusively in naming the postures. However, for those interested in the original names, we've included a list of many of the postures with their Sanskrit names and the page number on which they appear.

Posture	**Sanskrit Name**	**Page**
Bow	Dhanurasana	93
Bridge	Setu Bandhasana	162
Butterfly Cobbler	Upavistha Konasana	108
Camel	Supta Vajrasana	192
Cat Tilt	Marjariasana	88
Child's Pose	Balasana	113, 193
Cobra	Bhujangasana	60, 88

Posture	Sanskrit Name	Page
Corpse Pose	Savasana	133
Crow	Kakasana	151
Downward-Facing Dog	Adho Mukha Svanasana	60, 89
Eagle	Garudasana	148
Fish	Matsyasana	209
Forward Bend	Paschimothanasana	101
Half-Moon	Ardha-chandrasana	179
Headstand	Sirshasana	93
Incline Plane	Katikasana	204
Knee-Down Twist	Jathara Parivartanasana	133
Locust	Salabhasana	95
Mountain	Tadasana	45
Pigeon	Rajakapotasana	114
Plow	Halasana	161
Raindancer	Natarajasana	149
Revolving Triangle	Parivrtta Trikonasana	70
Scorpion	Vrischikasana	195
Shoulder Stand	Savangasana	160
Side Angle Pose	Uttitha Parsvakonasana	182
Spinal Twist	Ardha Matsyendrasana	115
Standing Forward Bend	Padahasthasana	57, 60
Standing Knee-to-Chest	Pavanmuktasana	146
Sun Salutation	Surya Namaskar	57
Tree	Vrksasana	145
Triangle	Trikonasana	69
Upward Boat	Navasana	92, 203
Warrior One	Virabhadrasana 1	45
Warrior Two	Virabhadrasana 2	46
Wheel	Chakrasana	162

Appendix C

What Science Says About Yoga

Yogic breathing exercises significantly improve pulmonary function and lower free-radical activity in healthy individuals, according to a study presented at Chest 2000, the annual meeting of the American College of Chest Physicians. Thirty healthy volunteers performed yogic breathing exercises for thirty minutes every day for ten weeks. Pulmonary function tests were done initially and at the end of the ten-week exercise period.

Levels of malonaldehyde (an indicator of free-radical activity) and superoxide dismutase (an indicator of antioxidant activity) were also collected. Following the exercise period, volunteers showed significant improvement in pulmonary function. Malonaldehyde levels also decreased significantly (9.54+/−0.56 nm/mL before exercises to 8.21+/−0.76 nm/mL after exercises). Superoxide dismutase levels increased, but not significantly (11.60+/−3.14 units/mg to 13.04+/−2.66).

Researchers concluded that the practice of yoga not only improves pulmonary lung function in healthy adults, but may also be helpful in reducing the prevalence of bronchial asthma, chronic obstructive pulmonary disease, and lung cancer.

Source: Kant S. Evaluation of yogic breathing exercises on pulmonary function, free radicals, and antioxidant status among healthy individuals. Presented at the annual meeting of the American College of Chest Physicians, October 25, 2000, San Francisco, CA.

Index

Page numbers in **boldface** refer to photographs or illustrations.